THE
SHERLOCK HOLMES
COMPANION

An early portrait of Sherlock Holmes by Sidney Paget

Reproduced by kind permission of Messrs. Whitbread & Co. Ltd.

THE
SHERLOCK HOLMES
COMPANION

◆

MICHAEL AND MOLLIE HARDWICK

ILLUSTRATIONS BY SIDNEY PAGET

BRAMHALL HOUSE • NEW YORK

This book
is dedicated to the living memory of
SIR ARTHUR CONAN DOYLE
in gratitude and admiration

FOREWORD

One thing which has struck us most forcibly while compiling *The Sherlock Holmes Companion* has been the illusion that we were dealing with a figure of real life rather than of fiction. How vital Holmes appears, compared with many people of one's own acquaintance! From how many eminent Lives could one distil so balanced a philosophy, so vivid a self-portrait, so penetrating a view of human nature and contemporary society? Compare Holmes's sayings with those of any public figure, Victorian or otherwise. Perhaps the same wisdom will be found, or the pungency of wit, or the perception—but seldom all together. It is as though the sensitive mind of Sir Arthur Conan Doyle, which was later to be so sincerely convinced of 'a world elsewhere', had unwittingly summoned from that world a spirit of such rare quality that it refused to return to the shadows, or to leave its sometimes unwilling master. Perhaps that other figure of vast reality, Falstaff, was such another spirit, and tormented Shakespeare as Holmes tormented Conan Doyle. Both were killed off in desperation by the men who had called them into being; and both were restored to life by the prayers of their worshippers.

This volume should, perhaps, more properly bear the title 'The Sherlock Holmes Reader's Companion'; for that is what it is intended to be. Our chief aim has been to tempt the uninitiated reader into the inevitable delight of reading all of Sherlock Holmes for himself, while at the same time to provide for the well versed a quick reference guide to more than two hundred significant characters, all sixty plots, and a good deal else, using only the information to be found in the text. We have resisted, as far as we could, the temptation to speculate upon chronology, geography, and those anomalies and inconsistencies which provide such rich material for the application of certain of Holmes's own methods. Anyone wishing to refresh his memory as to which story deals with the strange affair of young Cadogan West, who abruptly left his fiancée standing in a fog-bound street, never to be seen by her again, will find his answer here. If, troubled by a nagging half-recollection, someone should find himself in straits over the occupation of a certain Mr. Mordecai Smith, or the name of the partner in bigamy of Miss Hatty Doran, he can quickly find the answers here. Admittedly, in writing the biographies of Holmes and Watson we have permitted ourselves a certain latitude of inference and assumption. In summarizing the stories we have endeavoured to set the scenes and pose the problems without giving away too many details of the plots; a reservation which applies particularly to the *Who's Who* section, for, as Holmes himself found, "It is always awkward doing business with an alias."

Our warm thanks are due to Mr. Adrian Conan Doyle for his enthusiastic co-operation and good wishes; to Mr. Alan Robertson, our erudite fellow member of the Sherlock Holmes Society of London, for scrutinizing the manuscript; and to Messrs. George Newnes for permission to use the Sidney Paget illustrations, and Mr. Michael Holder, manager of their Press Services Department, for his good offices in this direction.

The date given after each entry in the section of story summaries refers to first publication in any form, whether in England or the United States.

Lest it be charged that our preoccupation with Holmes and Watson has seduced our thoughts away from their 'onlie begetter,' we hasten to say that nothing could be less true. We yield to none in admiration of Sir Arthur Conan Doyle as writer and as man. It would also be an omission not to pay tribute to Sidney Paget. We believe that this volume contains the widest selection of his definitive illustrations ever assembled outside the original *Strand Magazine*—and, of course, many more have had to be excluded. Paget died in 1908 and subsequent stories were ably illustrated by others. But, for us, Sidney Paget is always *the* illustrator.

It only remains for us, like Watson, to ask: "Has anything escaped us? We trust there is nothing of consequence which we have overlooked?"

MICHAEL AND MOLLIE HARDWICK

CONTENTS

WHO'S WHO

ACTON, MR., of Reigate, Surrey. Owner of one of the largest houses in his district, which was broken into just before Holmes's arrival to stay with Colonel Hayter. Engaged in litigation with Squire Cunningham, upon half of whose estate he believed himself to have a claim. "One of our country magnates."—Hayter, *The Reigate Squires*.

ADAIR, THE HON. RONALD, second son of the Earl of Maynooth. Shot through the head in his locked room at his home, 427, Park Lane, on March 30th, 1894, with a soft-nosed revolver bullet, fired from a specially adapted airgun. 'But how did he come by his death? No one could have climbed up to the window without leaving traces. Suppose a man had fired through the window, it would indeed be a remarkable shot who could with a revolver inflict so deadly a wound.'—Watson, *The Empty House*.

ADLER, IRENE. Former operatic contralto, born New Jersey, U.S.A., in 1858. While prima donna at the Imperial Opera of Warsaw she became closely associated with Wilhelm Gottsreich Sigismund von Ormstein, King of Bohemia. Subsequently she lived for some time at Briony Lodge, Serpentine Avenue, St. John's Wood, and married Godfrey Norton, a lawyer of the Inner Temple, later returning to the Continent. "The daintiest thing under a bonnet on this planet."—Holmes. 'To Sherlock Holmes she is always *the* woman.'—Watson, *A Scandal in Bohemia*.

ALTAMONT. Irish-American alias of Sherlock Holmes in *His Last Bow*. "Altamont has a nice taste in wines, and he took a fancy to my Tokay. He is a touchy fellow and needs humouring in small things."—Von Bork.

AMBERLEY, JOSIAH, of The Haven, Lewisham. Former partner in Brickfall and Amberley, manufacturers of

artistic materials. He retired in 1896 and married the
following year a wife twenty years his junior, who soon
afterwards disappeared, apparently in company with a Dr.
Ray Ernest. "A competence, a wife, leisure—it seemed a
straight road which lay before him. And yet within two
years he is, as you have seen, as broken and miserable a
creature as crawls beneath the sun."—Holmes, *The
Retired Colourman.*

AMES. Butler to John Douglas at the Manor House,
Birlstone, Sussex. 'A quaint, gnarled, dried-up person.'
—Watson, *The Valley of Fear.*

'ANGEL, HOSMER'. Cashier, of Leadenhall Street, City
of London, and fiancé of Mary Sutherland. He disappeared
on the morning of their intended wedding at St. Saviour's
Church, near King's Cross. "As far as the church door he
brought her, and then, as he could go no further, he conveniently vanished away by the old trick of stepping in at
one door of a four-wheeler, and out at the other."—
Holmes, *A Case of Identity.*

Hosmer Angel

ANNA ——. A Russian-born member of a Nihilist party, betrayed by her husband and condemned to Siberia before escaping to England. "She has a remarkably thick nose, with eyes which are set close upon either side of it. She has a puckered forehead, a peering expression, and probably rounded shoulders."—Holmes. 'At the best she could never have been handsome.'—Watson, *The Golden Pince-nez*.

ARMSTRONG, DR. LESLIE. One of the heads of Cambridge University Medical School, and a scientist of European reputation. "I have not seen a man who, if he turned his talents that way, was more calculated to fill the gap left by the illustrious Moriarty."—Holmes, *The Missing Three-Quarter*.

BAKER, HENRY. Owner of the lost goose in *The Blue Carbuncle*. Scholar and habitué of the Alpha Inn, near the British Museum. 'A touch of red in nose and cheeks, with a slight tremor of his extended hand, recalled Holmes' surmise as to his habits.'—Watson.

BAKER STREET IRREGULARS. 'The Baker Street division of the detective police force': a gang of street arabs who assisted Holmes on a number of occasions. (*A Study in Scarlet, The Sign of Four, The Crooked Man, The Disappearance of Lady Frances Carfax*.) "There's more work to be got out of one of those little beggars than out of a dozen of the force. The mere sight of an official-looking person seals men's lips. These youngsters, however, go everywhere, and hear everything."—Holmes, *A Study in Scarlet*.

BALDWIN, TED, alias Hargrave, member of Lodge 341, Vermissa Valley, Ancient Order of Freemen. Sometime suitor of Ettie Shafter. After serving a long term of

2—S.H.C

imprisonment for his part in the criminal activities of the Scowrers organization, he visited England, where he met his death by gunshot. 'A young fellow came swaggering in with the air of one who is the master. He was a handsome, dashing young man.' *The Valley of Fear.*

BANNISTER. Servant to Hilton Soames, at St. Luke's College, and formerly butler to the late Sir Jabez Gilchrist. "There is the man who sent me in the right path." —Gilchrist Jnr, *The Three Students.*

BARCLAY, JAMES. Colonel commanding 1st Battalion, the Royal Mallows (formerly 117th Foot). He rose from the rank of private and was commissioned for bravery in the Indian Mutiny. Married Nancy Devoy, daughter of a colour-sergeant. He was found dead in suspicious circumstances in his quarters at Aldershot. "He was a dashing, jovial old soldier in his usual mood, but there were occasions on which he seemed to show himself capable of considerable violence and vindictiveness. This side of his nature, however, appears never to have been turned towards his wife."—Holmes, *The Crooked Man.*

BARKER. Private investigator retained by the family of Dr. Ray Ernest, of Lewisham, to inquire into his mysterious disappearance. "He is my hated rival upon the Surrey shore. . . . He has several good cases to his credit." —Holmes, *The Retired Colourman.*

BARKER, CECIL JAMES. Bachelor (reputed) of Hales Lodge, Hampstead. Formerly partner with John Douglas in a gold-mining venture at Benito Canyon, California. A leading witness in the Birlstone Manor shooting case. 'He was cordial and intimate with Douglas, and he was no less friendly with his wife, a friendship which more than once seemed to cause some irritation to the husband, so

that even the servants were able to perceive his annoyance.'
—Watson, *The Valley of Fear*.

BARRYMORE, JOHN AND ELIZA, *née* Selden, a married
couple, butler and housekeeper to Sir Henry Baskerville,
of Baskerville Hall, Dartmoor, Devonshire, and formerly
to his late uncle, Sir Charles Baskerville, under whose
will they each inherited £500. Barrymore's father had
been caretaker at Baskerville Hall. "They have looked
after the Hall for four generations now. So far as I know,
he and his wife are as respectable a couple as any in the
country."—Dr. James Mortimer, *The Hound of the
Baskervilles*.

BASKERVILLE, SIR
HENRY. Baronet, born
circa 1859; nephew and
heir to the late Sir Charles
Baskerville, of Baskerville
Hall, Dartmoor, Devon-
shire. He followed a farm-
ing career in Canada in
his twenties, returning to
England in 1889 after his
uncle's mysterious death.
'A small, alert, dark-eyed
man about thirty years of
age, very sturdily built,

Sir Henry Baskerville

with thick black eyebrows, and a strong pugnacious face.'
—Watson. "There is no devil in hell, Mr. Holmes, and
there is no man upon earth who can prevent me from going
to the home of my own people."—Sir H. Baskerville,
The Hound of the Baskervilles.

BAYNES, inspector in the Surrey Constabulary, and
misogynist. In charge of investigations in March, 1892,

into the murder of Aloysius Garcia, on Oxshott Common, Surrey. "I must congratulate you, inspector, on handling so distinctive and instructive a case. Your powers, if I may say so without offence, seem superior to your opportunities."—Holmes, *Wisteria Lodge*.

BEDDINGTON. Famous forger and cracksman. Shortly after completing five years' penal servitude he was arrested for the murder of a watchman at Mawson & Williams', the City of London financial house, during the course of an attempted robbery in association with his brother who masqueraded as the brothers Arthur and Henry Pinner.— *The Stockbroker's Clerk*.

BELLAMY, MAUD. Daughter of Tom Bellamy, boat and bathing-cot proprietor, The Haven, Fulworth, Sussex. Fiancée of Fitzroy McPherson, on the staff at The Gables, near Fulworth. 'Maud Bellamy will always remain in my memory as a most complete and remarkable woman.'— Holmes, *The Lion's Mane*.

BELLINGER, LORD. Twice Prime Minister of Great Britain. 'The Premier sprang to his feet with that quick, fierce gleam of his deep-set eyes before which a Cabinet had cowered.'—Watson, *The Second Stain*.

BENNETT, TREVOR ('Jack'). Assistant to Prof. Presbury, of Camford University, and engaged to his daughter, Edith. 'He was a tall, handsome youth about thirty, well dressed and elegant, but with something in his bearing which suggested the shyness of the student rather than the self-possession of the man of the world.'—Watson, *The Creeping Man*.

BEPPO. Italian piecework man, employed by Morse Hudson, picture-dealer, of Kennington, and Gelder & Co., of Stepney. At one time a sculptor, he had descended to doing small jobs for art-dealers, had become well known as a ne'er-do-well amongst the Italian colony of Saffron Hill, and had taken to crime. Murderer of the Neapolitan cut-throat, Pietro Venucci. 'An alert, sharp-featured simian man with thick eyebrows, and a very peculiar projection of the lower part of the face like the muzzle of a baboon.'—Watson, *The Six Napoleons.*

BILLY. Page-boy at 221B, Baker Street. 'The young but very wise and tactful page, who had helped a little to fill up the gap of loneliness and isolation which surrounded the saturnine figure of the great detective.' *The Mazarin Stone.*

'BLESSINGTON'. Patron of Dr. Percy Trevelyan, whom he set up in practice at 403, Brook Street. Found murdered in his own apartments on the first floor. "I can read in a man's eye when it is his own skin that he is frightened for."—Holmes, *The Resident Patient.*

'BOONE, HUGH'. Well-known City of London match-seller during the 1880s. Arrested on suspicion of having

Hugh Boone

murdered Neville St. Clair in June, 1889. "A shock of orange hair, a pale face disfigured by a horrible scar, which by its contraction, has turned up the outer edge of his upper lip, a bull-dog chin, and a pair of very penetrating dark eyes, which present a singular contrast to the colour of his hair, all mark him out from amid the common crowd of mendicants."—Holmes, *The Man with the Twisted Lip*.

BRACKENSTALL, LADY, *née* Fraser, of Adelaide, South Australia, and widow of Sir Eustace Brackenstall, of the Abbey Grange, Marsham, Kent. 'Over one eye rose a hideous, plum-coloured swelling.'—Watson. "I suppose that it's no use my attempting to conceal that our marriage has not been a happy one."—Lady Brackenstall, *The Abbey Grange*.

BRADSTREET, INSPECTOR, of Scotland Yard and formerly attached to Bow Street Police Station. Concerned with Holmes in three cases: *The Man with the Twisted Lip*, *The Engineer's Thumb* and *The Blue Carbuncle*. 'A tall, stout official had come down the stone-flagged passage, in a peaked cap and frogged jacket.' —Watson, *The Man with the Twisted Lip*.

BRECKINRIDGE. Poultry-stall keeper in Covent Garden Market. "When you see a man with whiskers of that cut and the 'Pink 'Un' protruding out of his pocket, you can always draw him by a bet."—Holmes, *The Blue Carbuncle*.

BROWN, JOSIAH, of Laburnum Vale, Chiswick. Owner of one of the six busts of Napoleon, the theft of which led to the arrest on his doorstep of the Italian, Beppo. 'A jovial, rotund figure in shirt and trousers.'—Watson, *The Six Napoleons*.

BROWN, SILAS. Manager of Lord Backwater's training stable, Capleton, near Tavistock, Devonshire. Trainer of

Desborough, second favourite for the Wessex Cup (at 15 to 5). "A more perfect compound of the bully, coward and sneak than Master Silas Brown I have seldom met with."—Holmes, *Silver Blaze*.

BROWNER, JAMES. Steward in the *May Day* (Liverpool, Dublin & London Steam Packet Co.). Married Mary Cushing, who disappeared while boating off New Brighton with a friend. "He would always take drink when he was ashore, and a little drink would send him stark, staring mad."—Susan Cushing, *The Cardboard Box*.

Jim Browner

BRUNTON, RICHARD. Butler for twenty years to Reginald Musgrave at Hurlstone Manor, West Sussex. An ex-school-master, accomplished lin-guist and musician. Engaged to (1) Rachel Howells, (2) Janet Tregellis. "The butler of Hurlstone is always a thing that is remembered by all who visit us."—Musgrave, *The Musgrave Ritual*.

'BURNET, MISS'. Governess to the two children of Mr. Henderson, of High Gable, near Oxshott, Surrey. Alias of Signora Victor Durando, British-born widow of the late San Pedro Minister in London. 'She bore upon her aquiline and emaciated face the traces of some recent tragedy. Her head hung listlessly upon her breast, but as she raised it and turned her dull eyes upon us, I saw that her pupils were dark dots in the centre of the broad grey iris. She was drugged with opium.'—Watson, *Wisteria Lodge*.

CAIRNS, PATRICK. Harpooner (twenty-six voyages), formerly of the steam sealer *Sea Unicorn*. Arrested for murder in July, 1895. "This room is not well adapted for a cell, and Mr. Patrick Cairns occupies too large a portion of our carpet."—Holmes, *Black Peter*.

CANTLEMERE, LORD. In charge of Government inquiries into the disappearance of the Mazarin diamond. "I can get along with the Prime Minister, and I've nothing against the Home Secretary, who seemed a civil, obliging sort of man, but I can't stand his lordship."—Billy, the page-boy, *The Mazarin Stone*.

CAREY, CAPT. PETER. Former sealer and whaler. Commanded the steam whaler *Sea Unicorn*. Retired from the sea in 1884, aged thirty-nine, and in 1889 settled with his wife and daughter at Woodman's Lee, near Forest Row, Sussex, where he was found murdered with a harpoon in 1895. "You would go far before you found a more dangerous man than Peter Carey, and I have heard that he bore the same character when he commanded his ship. He was known in the trade as Black Peter."—Inspector Hopkins, *Black Peter*.

CARFAX, LADY FRANCES. Spinster and last survivor of the direct family of the Earl of Rufton. Kidnapped on her return to London from travelling on the Continent. "A rather pathetic figure, the Lady Frances, a beautiful woman, still in fresh middle age, and yet, by a strange chance, the last derelict of what only twenty years ago was a goodly fleet."—Holmes, *The Disappearance of Lady Frances Carfax*.

CARRUTHERS, ROBERT, of Chiltern Grange, Farnham, Surrey, employer of Miss Violet Smith as music teacher to his daughter. "My employer, Mr. Carruthers, takes a great deal of interest in me. We are thrown rather together. I play his accompaniments in the evening. He has never said anything . . . but a girl always knows."—Violet Smith, *The Solitary Cyclist*.

CARTWRIGHT. A fourteen-year-old district messenger employed by Holmes to trace a mutilated copy of *The Times*, which had been used to convey a warning message to Sir Henry Baskerville at the Northumberland Hotel. He later supplied Holmes with food and information upon the moor. "He has given me an extra pair of eyes upon a very active pair of feet."—Holmes, *The Hound of the Baskervilles*.

CHARPENTIER, ARTHUR. Sub-lieutenant, Royal Navy. Son of Madame Charpentier, widowed proprietress of Charpentier's Boarding Establishment, Torquay Terrace, and brother of Alice Charpentier. Arrested on suspicion of the murder of Enoch J. Drebber. "He is utterly innocent of it. . . . His high character, his profession, his antecedents would forbid it."—Mme Charpentier, *A Study in Scarlet*.

'CORAM, PROFESSOR', of Yoxley Old Place, near Chatham, Kent. An elderly invalid, engaged in the analysis of documents found in Coptic monasteries in Syria and Egypt. "Tobacco and my work—that is all that is left to me."—Coram, *The Golden Pince-nez*.

CROKER, CAPT. JACK. Master of the s.s. *Bass Rock* and former First Officer of the *Rock of Gibraltar* (Adelaide-Southampton Co.). 'There was not an officer in the fleet to touch him.'—Watson, *The Abbey Grange*.

CUBITT, ELSIE, *née* Patrick, wife of Hilton Cubitt, of Ridling Thorpe Manor, Norfolk, an English gentleman. The daughter of a Chicago gang-leader, and formerly fiancée of Abe Slaney, she broke away from her father and his dishonest associates and fled to England, where she was subsequently the recipient of the Dancing Men messages, which were shortly followed by the murder of her husband. "I have had some very disagreeable associations in my life; I wish to forget all about them."—Elsie Patrick, *The Dancing Men*.

CUNNINGHAM. One of the Reigate Squires, a Justice of the Peace with one son, Alec. His coachman, William Kirwan, was shot dead while apparently endeavouring to prevent a burglary. 'The one was an elderly man, with a strong, deep-lined, heavy-eyed face; the other a dashing young fellow, whose bright, smiling expression and showy dress were in strange contrast with the business which had brought us there.'—Watson, *The Reigate Squires*.

CUSHING, SARAH, of New Street, Wallington; late of Liverpool and Croydon. Spinster sister of Susan Cushing and Mary Browner. "I don't know now whether it was pure devilry on the

Susan Cushing

part of this woman, or whether she thought that she could turn me against my wife by encouraging her to misbehave. Anyway, she took a house just two streets off, and let lodgings to sailors."—James Browner, *The Cardboard Box*.

CUSHING, SUSAN, of Cross Street, Croydon. Spinster sister of Sarah Cushing and Mary Browner. Recipient through the post of a parcel containing two freshly-severed human ears. 'It is a rare event for her to receive anything through the post.'—Daily Chronicle, *The Cardboard Box*.

DAMERY, COLONEL SIR JAMES. Irish-born man of the world and unofficial diplomatist. "He has rather a reputation for arranging delicate matters which are to be kept out of the papers."—Holmes, *The Illustrious Client*.

'DARBYSHIRE, WILLIAM'. *See* STRAKER, JOHN.

DEVINE, MARIE, of 11, Rue de Trajan, Montpelier. Formerly personal maid to Lady Frances Carfax. Fiancée of Jules Vibart, head waiter of the National Hotel, Lausanne. 'She was a devoted creature.'—Watson, *The Disappearance of Lady Frances Carfax*.

DIXIE, STEVE. Negro boxer and criminal. Member of the Spencer John gang, and suspected of being involved in the killing of one Perkins outside the Holborn Bar. 'He would have been a comic figure if he had not been terrific.' —Watson, *The Three Gables*.

DODD, JAMES M. Stockbroker, of Throgmorton Street, City of London, and friend of Godfrey Emsworth. Volunteered for service in the South African war, and

served with the Middlesex Corps of the Imperial Yeomanry until demobilized after the end of hostilities.
"When a gentleman of virile appearance enters my room
with such tan upon his face as an English sun could never
give, and with his handkerchief in his sleeve instead of in
his pocket, it is not difficult to place him."—Holmes, *The
Blanched Soldier*.

DOLORES. Peruvian maid to Mrs. Robert Ferguson at
Cheeseman's, Lamberley, Sussex, and before her marriage.
"The too faithful Dolores."—Holmes, *The Sussex Vampire*.

DORAN, HATTY. Only daughter of Aloysius Doran, of
San Francisco, and wife of Francis Hay Moulton. An
heiress, married (bigamously) to Lord St. Simon at St.
George's Church, Hanover Square, in 1887. "She is what
we call in England a tomboy, with a strong nature, wild
and free, unfettered by any sort of traditions."—Lord St.
Simon, *The Noble Bachelor*.

'DOUGLAS, JOHN'. Irish-born tenant of the Manor
House, Birlstone, Sussex. Sometime gold miner of Benito
Canyon, California, and former Pinkerton detective
Birdy Edwards (alias John McMurdo). His first wife
(*née* Shafter) died in California some years after their
marriage. Survived by his second wife, Ivy, when lost
overboard from s.s. *Palmyra* off St. Helena during a
voyage to South Africa. 'He was cheery and genial to all,
but somewhat offhand in his manners, giving the impression that he had seen life in social strata on some far
lower horizon than the county society of Sussex.'—
Watson, *The Valley of Fear*.

DREBBER, ENOCH J., of Cleveland, Ohio, and Salt Lake
City, Utah. Principal Elder of the Church of Latter Day
Saints, and husband of the late Lucy Ferrier. Found

murdered in an empty house off the Brixton Road, London. "After twelve o'clock in the day he could hardly ever be said to be sober. His manners towards the maid-servants were disgustingly free and familiar. Worst of all, he speedily assumed the same attitude towards my daughter, Alice, and spoke to her more than once in a way which, fortunately, she is too innocent to understand."—Mme Charpentier, *A Study in Scarlet*.

DUNBAR, GRACE. Governess to the two children of J. Neil Gibson, of Thor Place, Hampshire. 'A brunette, tall, with a noble figure and commanding presence.'—Watson. Arrested for the murder of Mrs. Neil Gibson. "She is a wonderfully fine woman in every way. He may well have wished his wife out of the road."—Sergeant Coventry, *Thor Bridge*.

ECCLES, JOHN SCOTT, of Popham House, Lee, Kent. A bachelor acquaintance of Aloysius Garcia, at whose home he was staying at the time of Garcia's murder in 1892. 'His life history was written in his heavy features and pompous manner. From his spats to his gold-rimmed spectacles he was a Conservative, a Churchman, a good citizen, orthodox and conventional to the last degree.'—Watson, *Wisteria Lodge*.

'EDWARDS, BIRDY'. Pinkerton detective (alias John McMurdo). *See* DOUGLAS, JOHN.

ELMAN, REV. J. C., M.A., vicar of Mossmoor-cum-Little Purlington, near Frinton, Essex. 'A big, solemn, rather pompous clergyman.'—Watson, *The Retired Colourman*.

EMSWORTH, COLONEL, V.C., of Tuxbury Old Park, near Bedford. He gained his Victoria Cross for valour during the Crimean campaign. Father of Godfrey Emsworth, whose disappearance was the subject of investigation by Sherlock Holmes. "A red-veined nose jutted out like a vulture's beak, and two fierce grey eyes glared at me from under tufted brows. I could understand now why Godfrey seldom spoke of his father."—James M. Dodd, *The Blanched Soldier*.

EMSWORTH, GODFREY. Son of Colonel Emsworth, v.c. Served as a volunteer with B Squadron, Middlesex Corps, Imperial Yeomanry, in the South African War (lance-corporal), until wounded (elephant gunshot) near Diamond Hill, Pretoria, in 1902. 'His appearance was certainly extraordinary. One could see that he had indeed been a handsome man with clear-cut features sunburned by an African sun, but mottled in patches over this darker surface were curious whitish patches which had bleached his skin.'—Holmes, *The Blanched Soldier*.

FAIRBAIRN, ALEC. Ex-seafaring man who disappeared while boating off New Brighton in a mist with a lady friend. "He had wonderful polite ways with him for a sailor man, so that I think there must have been a time when he knew more of the poop than the forecastle."—James Browner, *The Cardboard Box*.

'FERGUSON'. Alias of Dr. Becher, of Eyford, Berkshire, posing as secretary and manager to Colonel Lysander Stark. "A short, thick man with a chinchilla beard growing out of the creases of his double chin."—Victor Hatherley, *The Engineer's Thumb*.

FERGUSON, ROBERT, of Cheeseman's, Lamberley, Sussex, and of Ferguson and Muirhead, tea brokers, of Mincing Lane. One son, Jacky, by his first wife, and one (infant victim of vampirism) by his second. An old acquaintance of Watson's on the Rugby football field.

"Hullo, Watson—you don't look quite the man you did when I threw you over the ropes into the crowd at the Old Deer Park."—Ferguson, *The Sussex Vampire*.

FERGUSON, MRS. Second wife of Robert Ferguson and mother of his infant son. Daughter of a Peruvian merchant; Roman Catholic, beauty, and suspected vampire. "She is very jealous—jealous with all the strength of her fiery tropical love."—Robert Ferguson, *The Sussex Vampire*.

FERRIER, JOHN. Farmer and member of the Church of Latter Day Saints, Salt Lake City, Utah. Shot to death on August 4th, 1860, while escaping with his daughter from the settlement. 'From the great inland sea to the distant Wahsatch Mountains there was no name better known than that of John Ferrier.' *A Study in Scarlet*.

FERRIER, LUCY. Adopted daughter of John Ferrier. Married to Enoch J. Drebber, but died within a month of her marriage. Her wedding ring was found in Brixton, London, in 1881. 'Many a wayfarer upon the high road which ran by Ferrier's farm felt long-forgotten thoughts revive in their minds as they watched her lithe, girlish figure tripping through the wheatfields, or met her mounted upon her father's mustang, and managing it with all the ease and grace of a true child of the West.' *A Study in Scarlet*.

FORRESTER, INSPECTOR. Surrey police officer who investigated the shooting of William Kirwan. 'A smart, keen-faced young fellow.'—Watson, *The Reigate Squires*.

FRANKLAND. Occupant of Lafter Hall, Dartmoor, Devonshire, and neighbour of the Baskerville family. Amateur astronomer, student of old manorial and communal rights, and habitual litigant. 'He is said to have about seven lawsuits upon his hands at present.' *The Hound of the Baskervilles*.

GARCIA, ALOYSIUS. Son of the former highest dignitary of the South American Republic of San Pedro. At the time of his murder, on Oxshott Common, Surrey, he was attached to the Spanish Embassy in London and residing at Wisteria Lodge, near Esher. "The deceased Garcia had a scheming mind and a well-developed instinct of self-preservation."—Holmes, *Wisteria Lodge*.

'GARRIDEB, JOHN', Counsellor at Law, of Moorville, Kansas. Alias of James Winter, alias Morecroft, alias 'Killer' Evans, of Chicago, murderer. Escaped from U.S.A. and arrived in London in 1893. Killed (in self defence) the Chicago forger and coiner, Rodger Prescott, in a night club in the Waterloo Road in 1895. Sentenced to five years' imprisonment and released in 1901. Subsequently imprisoned again. "Very dangerous man, usually carries arms and is prepared to use them. That is our bird, Watson—a sporting bird, as you must admit." —Holmes, *The Three Garridebs*.

GARRIDEB, NATHAN. Naturalist, archaeologist and collector, of 136, Little Ryder Street, London, W. Expectant beneficiary under the will of the late Alexander Hamilton Garrideb, of Kansas, U.S.A., who left his property to be divided equally between any three adult males named Garrideb. Last heard of in a Brixton nursing-home. "Just think what I could do with five million dollars. . . . I shall be the Hans Sloane of my age."— Nathan Garrideb, *The Three Garridebs*.

GIBSON, J. NEIL, of Thor Place, Hampshire. Gold-mining magnate and former senator for one of the Western States of the U.S.A. Married Maria Pinto, daughter of a

Brazilian government official, who was found shot in the grounds of their home. 'An Abraham Lincoln keyed to base uses instead of high ones would give some idea of the man.'—Watson, *Thor Bridge*.

GILCHRIST. Student at St. Luke's College. Rugby player, cricketer, Blue for hurdles and long-jump. Son of the late Sir Jabez Gilchrist, well known in racing circles. "My scholar has been left very poor, but he is hard-working and industrious."—Hilton Soames, *The Three Students*.

GORGIANO, GIUSEPPE ('Black Gorgiăno'). A leading official of the notorious Red Circle, a Neapolitan society allied to the old Carbonari, specializing in blackmail and murder. Found dead in a flat in Great Orme Street, London. "The giant Gorgiano, a man who had earned the name of 'Death' in the South of Italy."—Emilia Lucca, *The Red Circle*.

GREEN, THE HON. PHILIP, c/o the Langham Hotel, Portland Place, formerly of Barberton, South Africa. Son of Admiral Sir Philip Green, Bart. Former friend of Lady Frances Carfax. "Un sauvage—un véritable sauvage!"— Jules Vibart. 'Through the open sitting-room window I saw a huge, swarthy man with a bristling black beard walking slowly down the centre of the street. . . . Acting upon the impulse of the moment, I rushed out and accosted him. "You are an Englishman," I said.'—Watson, *The Disappearance of Lady Frances Carfax*.

GREGORY, INSPECTOR. Police officer in charge of the Silver Blaze case. 'A tall fair man with lion-like hair and beard, and curiously penetrating light blue eyes . . . a man who was rapidly making his name in the English detective service.'—Watson. "See the value of imagination. It is the one quality which Gregory lacks."—Holmes, *Silver Blaze*.

GREGSON, TOBIAS. Police inspector, regarded by Holmes as the smartest member of Scotland Yard. "He and Lestrade are the pick of a bad lot." Concerned in the cases of *A Study in Scarlet*, *The Greek Interpreter*, *The Red Circle* and *Wisteria Lodge*. 'A tall, white-faced, flaxen-haired man, with a note-book in his hand.'—Watson, *A Study in Scarlet*.

GRUNER, BARON ADELBERT. Austrian-born horse fancier, collector of books, pictures and women. Author of a standard work upon Ming china. Compiler of the 'lust diary': "This horrible book,"—Sir James Damery; "A beastly book—a book no man, even if he had come from the gutter, could have put together."—Kitty Winter. "The fellow is, as you may have heard, extraordinarily handsome, with a most fascinating manner, a gentle voice, and that air of romance and mystery which means so much to a woman. He is said to have the whole sex at his mercy and to have made ample use of the fact."—Sir James Damery, *The Illustrious Client*. Disfigured with vitriol at his home, Vernon Lodge, near Kingston.

HARKER, HORACE. Journalist with the Central Press Syndicate. The murdered Italian, Pietro Venucci, was found on his doorstep at 131, Pitt Street. "All my life I have been collecting other people's news, and now that a real piece of news has come my way I am so confused and bothered that I can't quite put two words together."—Harker, *The Six Napoleons*.

HARRISON, JOSEPH. Son of a North of England iron-master. Brother of Annie Harrison and prospective brother-in-law of Percy Phelps. 'His age may have been nearer forty than thirty, but his cheeks were so ruddy and his eyes so merry, that he still conveyed the impression of a plump and mischievous boy.'—Watson. "I am afraid

Joseph's character is a rather deeper and more dangerous one than one might judge from his appearance."—Holmes, *The Naval Treaty*.

HARRISON, ANNIE. Fiancée of Percy Phelps, of Briarbrae, Woking, and sister of Joseph Harrison. 'She was a striking-looking woman, a little short and thick for symmetry, but with a beautiful olive complexion, large, dark Italian eyes, and a wealth of deep black hair.'—Watson, *The Naval Treaty*.

HATHERLEY, VICTOR. Victim of a murderous assault, resulting in the loss of his thumb. Orphan, bachelor, and unsuccessful hydraulic engineer of 16A, Victoria Street. "During two years I have had three consultations and one small job. . . . My gross takings amount to twenty-seven pounds ten."—Hatherley, *The Engineer's Thumb*.

Joseph Harrison

HAYES, REUBEN. Landlord of the Fighting Cock Inn. near Mackleton, Derbyshire. Formerly head coachman to the sixth Duke of Holdernesse, and associate of James

Wilder, secretary to the duke. "A more self-evident villain I never saw."—Holmes, *The Priory School*.

HAYTER, COLONEL. Former army officer and friend of Dr. Watson. Holmes's and Watson's host at his home near Reigate, Surrey, following the Netherland-Sumatra Company affair of 1887. 'A little diplomacy was needed, but when Holmes understood that the establishment was a bachelor

Victor Hatherley

one, and that he would be allowed the fullest freedom, he fell in with my plans.'—Watson, *The Reigate Squires*.

'HENDERSON'. Alias of the deposed Central American dictator, Don Juan Murillo, 'The Tiger of San Pedro', while living at High Gable, near Oxshott, Surrey. Believed murdered by persons unknown late in 1892 at the Hotel Escurial, Madrid, where he was known as the Marquess of Montalva. 'The most lewd and bloodthirsty tyrant that had ever governed any country with a pretence to civilisation.'—Watson, *Wisteria Lodge*.

HOLDER, ALEXANDER. Senior partner in the second largest private bankers in the City of London, Holder & Stevenson, of Threadneedle Street, who advanced £50,000 to "one of the highest, noblest, most exalted names in England" against security of the priceless Beryl Coronet. 'His actions were in absurd contrast to the dignity of his dress and features, for he was running hard, with occasional little springs, such as a weary man gives who is little accustomed to set any tax upon his legs.'—Watson, *The Beryl Coronet*.

HOLDER, ARTHUR. Son of Alexander Holder. Given in charge by his father for the attempted theft of the Beryl Coronet at their home, Fairbank, Streatham. "He has been a grievous disappointment to me, Mr. Holmes, a grievous disappointment." —Alexander Holder, *The Beryl Coronet*.

HOLDER, MARY. Niece of Alexander Holder. She eloped with the notorious Sir George Burnwell. "My little Mary, who has a woman's quick insight into character." — Alexander Holder, *The Beryl Coronet*.

HOLDERNESSE, SIXTH DUKE OF, K.G., P.C., etc. Baron Beverley, Earl of Carston, Lord-Lieutenant of Hallamshire from 1900, Lord of the Admiralty, 1872, etc., etc. Married (1888) Edith, daughter of Sir Charles Appledore. Heir, Lord Saltire. "His Grace is not in the habit of posting letters himself."— James Wilder, *The Priory School*.

The Duke of Holdernesse

HOLDHURST, LORD. Conservative Foreign Secretary. Uncle of Percy Phelps, Holmes's client in the affair of *The Naval Treaty*. "He's a fine fellow. But he has a struggle to keep up his position. . . . You noticed, of course, that his boots had been re-soled?"— Holmes.

HOLMES, MYCROFT. Elder brother, by seven years, of Sherlock Holmes. Government accountant and inter-departmental adviser. "Mycroft draws four hundred and fifty pounds a year, remains a subordinate, has no ambitions of any kind, will receive neither honour nor title, but remains the most indispensable man in the country."—Holmes, *The Bruce-Partington Plans*. Residence: lodgings in Pall Mall. "He walks round the corner into Whitehall every morning and back every evening. From year's end to year's end he takes no other exercise."—Holmes, *The Greek Interpreter*. Founder member of the Diogenes Club,

Lord Holdhurst

Pall Mall. "It now contains the most unsociable and un-clubbable men in town."—Holmes, *The Greek Interpreter*. Respected by Holmes for his (wasted) powers of observation and deduction. "If the art of the detective began and ended in reasoning from an arm-chair, my brother would be the greatest criminal agent that ever lived. But he has no ambition and no energy. He would not even go out of his way to verify his own solutions, and would

Mycroft Holmes

rather be considered wrong than take the trouble to prove himself right." *The Greek Interpreter*. Much larger and stouter than his brother. "It is as if you met a tram-car coming down a country lane."—Holmes, *The Bruce-Partington Plans*. Appears in *The Greek Interpreter*, *The Bruce-Partington Plans*, *The Final Problem*.

HOPE, THE RT. HON. TRELAWNEY. Secretary for European Affairs. Private residence, Whitehall Terrace. 'His handsome face was distorted with a spasm of despair, and his hands tore at his hair. For a moment we caught a glimpse of the natural man—impulsive, ardent, keenly sensitive.'—Watson, *The Second Stain*.

HOPE, LADY HILDA TRELAWNEY. Wife of the Rt. Hon. Trelawney Hope, and daughter of the Duke of Belminster. 'A moment later our modest apartment, already so distinguished that morning, was further honoured by the entrance of the most lovely woman in London.'—Watson, *The Second Stain.*

HOPE, JEFFERSON. Californian pioneer, scout, trapper, prospector for silver, ranchman, hunter, and, in March, 1881, registered London cab-driver. Died in custody in London. 'Year passed into year, his black hair turned grizzled, but still he wandered on, a human bloodhound, with his mind wholly set upon the one object to which he had devoted his life.' *A Study in Scarlet.*

HOPKINS, STANLEY. Police inspector, of 46, Lord Street, Brixton, associated with the cases of *The Golden Pince-nez, Black Peter, The Missing Three-Quarter, The Abbey Grange.* At the time of the *Black Peter* case he was only thirty, and Holmes held high, though fluctuating, hopes for his future. "I am disappointed in Stanley Hopkins. I had hoped for better things from him."

HOWELLS, RACHEL. Second housemaid to Reginald Musgrave at Hurlstone Manor, West Sussex. Formerly engaged to the butler, Richard Brunton. "Rachel, who is a very good girl, but of an excitable Welsh temperament, had a sharp touch of brain fever, and goes about the house now—or did until yesterday—like a black-eyed shadow of her former self."—Musgrave, *The Musgrave Ritual.*

HUDSON. Former seaman, of no fixed abode. A survivor, in his youth, of the wrecked convict transport *Gloria Scott,* in whose crew he was serving when she disappeared on passage from Falmouth to Australia in 1855. Subsequently employed as gardener, and later as butler, by James Trevor, J.P. "The maids complained of his drunken habits and his vile language. The dad raised their wages all round to recompense them for the annoyance."—Victor Trevor, *The 'Gloria Scott.'*

HUDSON, MORSE. Dealer in pictures and statuary, of Kennington Road. The smashing of a bust of Napoleon in his shop by an unidentified man began the train of events in the case of *The Six Napoleons*. 'He was a small, stout man with a red face and a peppery manner.'—Watson.

HUDSON, MRS. Holmes's and Watson's landlady at 221B, Baker Street. "Her cuisine is a little limited, but she has as good an idea of breakfast as a Scotchwoman."—Holmes, *The Naval Treaty*. 'Not only was her first-floor flat invaded at all hours by throngs of singular and often undesirable characters, but her remarkable lodger showed an eccentricity and irregularity in his life which must have sorely tried her patience. His incredible untidiness, his addiction to music at strange hours, his occasional revolver practice within doors, his weird and often malodorous scientific experiments, and the atmosphere of violence and danger which hung around him made him the very worst tenant in London.'—Watson, *The Dying Detective*. She appears in *The Sign of Four*, *The Naval Treaty*, *The Empty House*, *Black Peter*, *The Valley of Fear*, *The Mazarin Stone*, *His Last Bow*, *The Speckled Band*, *The Dying Detective*, *Wisteria Lodge*, *The Lion's Mane*, *A Scandal in Bohemia*, *The Second Stain*, *The Three Garridebs*.

HUNTER, VIOLET. An orphan, employed for five years as governess to the family of Colonel Spence Munro until their departure for Nova Scotia. She then obtained, through Westaway's agency, a situation as governess to the son of Jephro Rucastle, of The Copper Beeches, near Winchester, but consulted Holmes about the unusual terms of her engagement. "I confess that it is not the situation which I should like to see a sister of mine apply for."— Holmes. 'She was plainly but neatly dressed, with a bright, quick face, freckled like a plover's egg, and with the brisk manner of a woman who has had her own way to make in the world.' — Watson, *The Copper Beeches*.

HUXTABLE, DR. THORNEYCROFT, M.A., Ph.D., etc., founder and principal of the Priory School, near Mackleton, Derbyshire. Author of *Hux-table's Sidelights on Horace*. 'His card, which seemed too small to carry the weight of his academic distinctions, preceded him by a few seconds, and then he entered himself—so large, so pompous, and so dignified that he was the very embodiment of self-possession and solidity. And yet his first action when the door had closed behind him was to stagger against the table, whence he slipped down upon the floor, and there was that majestic figure prostrate and insensible upon our bearskin hearthrug.'—Watson, *The Priory School*.

Violet Hunter

JOHNSON, SHINWELL ('Porky'). Ex-convict engaged by Holmes to supply information about the criminal underworld. 'With the glamour of his two convictions upon him, he had the *entrée* of every night club, doss house and gambling den in the town.'—Watson, *The Illustrious Client*.

JOHNSON, SIDNEY. Senior clerk and draughtsman in the Submarine Section at Woolwich Arsenal at the time of the theft of the Bruce-Partington plans. "The place is disorganised. The Chief dead, Cadogan West dead, our papers stolen. And yet, when we closed our door on Monday evening we were as efficient an office as any in the Government service."— Johnson, *The Bruce-Partington Plans.*

JONES, ATHELNEY. Scotland Yard detective officially credited with the solution of the case of *The Sign of Four.* 'He was red-faced, burly, and plethoric, with a pair of very small, twinkling eyes, which looked keenly out from between swollen and puffy pouches.'—Watson. "When Gregson, or Lestrade, or Athelney Jones are out of their depths—which, by the way, is their normal state—the matter is laid before me."—Holmes.

Dr. Thorneycroft Huxtable

JONES, PETER. Official police agent associated with Holmes in the case of *The Red-headed League.* "He is not a bad fellow, though an absolute imbecile in his profession."—Holmes.

KIRWAN, WILLIAM. Coachman to Mr. Cunningham, J.P., of Reigate. Shot dead while apparently trying to prevent a burglary at his master's house. "Shot through the heart, sir, and never spoke again."—Colonel Hayter's butler, *The Reigate Squires.*

KLEIN, ISADORA. Widow of Klein, the German sugar king. A celebrated beauty, born into the Pernambucan aristocracy, of pure Spanish descent. "The richest as well as the most lovely widow upon earth. . . . But she is the *'belle dame sans merci'* of fiction."—Holmes. Mistress of the late Douglas Maberley. "There was an interval of adventure when she pleased her own tastes."—Holmes, *The Three Gables.*

KRATIDES, PAUL AND SOPHY. A Greek brother and sister, of a wealthy Athenian family, who fell into the clutches of the notorious Wilson Kemp and Harold Latimer, by whom Paul Kratides was subsequently murdered. "Their embrace was but for an instant, however, for the younger man seized the woman and pushed her out of the room, while the elder easily overpowered his emaciated victim, and dragged him away through the other door."—Melas, *The Greek Interpreter.*

LANNER, INSPECTOR. Police officer investigating the suicide of Mr. Blessington at 403, Brook Street. 'A smart-looking police inspector.'—Watson, *The Resident Patient.*

LATIMER, HAROLD. Kidnapper, with Wilson Kemp, 'a man of the foulest antecedents', of Paul Kratides, the brother of a Greek girl with whom he had formed an attachment. Latimer and Kemp were subsequently believed to

Harold Latimer

have stabbed one another to death while travelling in Hungary with Sophy Kratides. 'Holmes, however, is, I fancy, of a different way of thinking, and he holds to this day that if one could find the Grecian girl one might learn how the wrongs of herself and her brother came to be avenged.'—Watson, *The Greek Interpreter*.

LESTRADE, G., Scotland Yard inspector, concerned in thirteen of Holmes's cases: *The Cardboard Box, The Norwood Builder, A Study in Scarlet, The Six Napoleons, The Hound of the Baskervilles, The Second Stain, The Boscombe Valley Mystery, The Bruce-Partington Plans, Charles Augustus Milverton, The Empty House, The Disappearance of Lady Frances Carfax, The Noble Bachelor, The Three Garridebs*. A quick and energetic worker, despite his adherence to conventional methods to

Inspector Lestrade

the exclusion of inspiration, and regarded by Holmes as comparable with only Gregson at the Yard. 'There was one sallow, rat-faced, dark-eyed fellow, who was introduced to me as Lestrade.'—Watson, *A Study in Scarlet*.

LEVERTON. Investigator, of Pinkerton's Agency (U.S.A.). Hero of the Long Island Cave Mystery. Visited London in pursuit of Giuseppe Gorgiano, 'A quiet, business-like young man, with a clean shaven, hatchet face.'—Watson, *The Red Circle*.

LUCAS, EDUARDO, of Godolphin Street, Westminster, where he was found stabbed to death at the age of thirty-four. Society man, unmarried, and one of the best amateur tenors in the country. Spent much of his life in Paris, where he was known as Henri Fournaye, sharing a small villa in the Rue Austerlitz with 'Mme Henri Fournaye', a Creole of excitable temperament. "He kept his life in watertight compartments."—Lestrade, *The Second Stain*.

LUCCA, EMILIA. Born Posilippo, near Naples, daughter of chief deputy Augusto Barelli. Married to Gennaro Lucca, fugitive in London from the Neapolitan society, The Red Circle. 'There, framed in the doorway, was a tall and beautiful woman—the mysterious lodger of Bloomsbury.'—Watson, *The Red Circle*.

LYONS, LAURA, of Coombe Tracey, Dartmoor, Devonshire. Daughter of Frankland, friend and neighbour of the late Sir Charles Baskerville. Deserted by her artist husband and cast off by her father, she was helped by Sir Charles Baskerville, John Stapleton and Dr. James Mortimer to earn her living. 'There was something subtly wrong with the face, some coarseness of expression, some hardness, perhaps, of eye, some looseness of lip which marred its perfect beauty.'—Watson, *The Hound of the Baskervilles*.

MABERLEY, MARY, of the Three Gables, Harrow Weald. Widow of Mortimer Maberley and mother of the late Douglas Maberley, British Attaché at Rome and minor novelist. After her son's death she led a retired life at her home, until the receipt of a mysterious offer from a house agent named Haines-Johnson caused her to seek Holmes's advice. "You gave me good advice, Mr. Holmes. Alas, I did not take it!" *The Three Gables*.

McCARTHY, CHARLES. Widower, tenant of Hatherley Farm, near Ross-on-Wye, Herefordshire, and former wagon-driver. Murdered with a blunt instrument beside Boscombe Pool, close to his farm. "A man of a very violent temper."—James McCarthy, evidence at inquest. *The Boscombe Valley Mystery*.

McCARTHY, JAMES. Only son of Charles McCarthy. Married (bigamously) to a Bristol barmaid. Committed to Herefordshire Assizes on suspicion of having murdered his father. "He is not a very quick-witted youth, though comely to look at, and, I should think, sound at heart."— Holmes, *The Boscombe Valley Mystery*.

MACDONALD, ALEC. Scotland Yard inspector. An Aberdonian, he achieved distinction in a number of investigations early in his career, and is officially credited with the solution of the mystery at Birlstone Manor, Sussex. 'The affection and respect of the Scotchman for his amateur colleague were profound, and he showed them by the frankness with which he consulted Holmes in every difficulty.'—Watson, *The Valley of Fear*.

McFARLANE, JOHN HECTOR, of Torrington Lodge, Blackheath. Bachelor, solicitor, freemason, and asthmatic. Junior partner in the firm of Graham & McFarlane, 426, Gresham Buildings. Arrested on suspicion of having murdered Jonas Oldacre. "I am nearly mad, Mr. Holmes, I am the unhappy John Hector McFarlane." *The Norwood Builder*.

McGINTY, JOHN ('Black Jack'). Saloon keeper and councillor of Vermissa, U.S.A. Bodymaster of Lodge 341, Vermissa Valley, Ancient Order of Freemen, and Boss of the Scowrers, a breakaway group of the A.O.F. devoted to murder and other crimes. Hanged with eight of his chief followers. "Drink and politics had made the Boss a very rich as well as powerful man." *The Valley of Fear*.

McLaren, Miles. Student at St. Luke's College. "He is a brilliant fellow when he chooses to work—one of the brightest intellects of the University: but he is wayward, dissipated, and unprincipled."—Hilton Soames, *The Three Students*.

'McMurdo, John.' Member of the Scowrers of Pennsylvania. *See* Douglas, John.

McPherson, Fitzroy. Science master at The Gables scholastic coaching establishment near Fulworth, Sussex. Fiancé of Miss Maud Bellamy, of The Haven, Fulworth. Died in mysterious circumstances after swimming, July, 1907. "I knew Mr. McPherson well enough to be aware that he was a brave and a strong man."—Maud Bellamy, *The Lion's Mane*.

Marvin, Teddy. Captain of the Coal and Iron Police, Vermissa Valley, U.S.A., and formerly of Chicago Central. "What are you but the paid tool of the men of capital, hired by them to club or to shoot your poorer fellow-citizens?"—Bodymaster McGinty, *The Valley of Fear*.

Mason, John. Head trainer to Sir Robert Norberton, the horse breeder. He consulted Holmes after discovering the upper condyle of a human femur in a furnace at his place of employment. 'A tall, clean-shaven man with the firm, austere expression which is only seen upon those who have to control horses or boys.'—Watson, *Shoscombe Old Place*.

Mason, White. Chief detective of the Sussex Constabulary. He investigated the shooting of John Douglas at the Manor House, Birlstone. "White Mason is a smart man. No local job has ever been too much for White Mason."—Sgt. Wilson, *The Valley of Fear*.

Melas. A Greek-born linguistic expert, lodging in apartments above those in Pall Mall of Mycroft Holmes, and a fellow member of his club, the Diogenes. Abducted on two occasions by Harold Latimer and forcibly detained at The Myrtles, Beckenham. "He earns his living partly as interpreter in the law courts, partly by acting as guide to any wealthy Orientals who may use the Northumberland Avenue hotels."—Mycroft Holmes, *The Greek Interpreter*.

MERTON, SAM. Boxer and associate of Count Negretto Sylvius, described by Holmes as the gudgeon to Sylvius' shark. "Billy, you will see a large and ugly gentleman outside the front door. Ask him to come up."—Holmes, *The Mazarin Stone*.

Melas

DE MERVILLE, VIOLET. Daughter of General de Merville, living with him at 104, Berkeley Square, where he had settled in retirement after a notable career and distinguished service in the Khyber Pass. Her father's health and strength were much affected by her romantic attachment to the notorious Baron Gruner. "She is beautiful, but with the ethereal other-world beauty of some fanatic whose thoughts are set on high. . . . How a man-beast could have laid his vile paws upon such a being of the beyond I cannot imagine. You may have noticed how extremes call to each other, the spiritual to the animal, the cave-man to the angel. You never saw a worse case than this."—Holmes, *The Illustrious Client*.

4—S.H.C.

MILLAR, FLORA. Former *danseuse* at The Allegro and friend of Lord St. Simon. Arrested after causing a disturbance at the wedding breakfast of Lord St. Simon and Hatty Doran. "Flora was a dear little thing, but exceedingly hot-headed, and devotedly attached to me."—Lord St. Simon, *The Noble Bachelor*.

MILVERTON, CHARLES AUGUSTUS. "The worst man in London . . . the king of all the blackmailers."—Holmes. Killed, aged fifty, at his home, Appledore Towers, Hampstead, by an unnamed woman. "Do you feel a creeping, shrinking sensation, Watson, when you stand before the serpents in the Zoo and see the slithery, gliding, venomous creatures, with their deadly eyes and wicked, flattened faces? Well, that's how Milverton impresses me. I've had to do with fifty murderers in my career, but the worst of them never

Charles Augustus Milverton

gave me the repulsion which I have for this fellow."—Holmes, *Charles Augustus Milverton*.

MORAN, COLONEL SEBASTIAN. "The second most dangerous man in London."—Holmes. Born in London, 1840, son of Sir Augustus Moran, C.B., former British Minister to Persia. Educated at Eton and Oxford. Served in the Jowaki and Afghan Campaigns, at Charasiab (mentioned in despatches), Sherpur and Cabul. Crack shot and gambler. Author of *Heavy Game of the Western Himalayas*, 1881; *Three Months in the Jungle*, 1884. Address: Conduit Street. Clubs: Anglo-Indian, Tankerville, Bagatelle Card Club. Sometime chief of staff to Professor Moriarty. 'With the brow of a philosopher above and the jaw of a sensualist below, the man must have started with great capacities for good or for evil. But one could not look upon his cruel blue eyes, with their drooping, cynical lids, or upon the fierce, aggressive nose and the threatening, deep-lined brow, without reading Nature's plainest danger-signals.' — Watson, *The Empty House.*

Colonel Sebastian Moran

MORIARTY, PROFESSOR JAMES. "The Napoleon of crime . . . organizer of half that is evil and nearly all that is undetected in this great city. He is a genius, a philosopher, an abstract thinker."—Holmes, *The Final Problem.* Of good birth and excellent education. Author of *The Dynamics of an Asteroid*—"a book which ascends to such rarefied heights of pure mathematics that it is said that there was no man in the scientific press capable of criticizing it."—Holmes, *The Valley of Fear.* At the age of twenty-one he wrote a treatise upon the Binomial Theorem which enjoyed a European vogue and earned him the Chair of Mathematics at one of the smaller British universities. Rumours connected with his name compelled him to relinquish this and he set up in London as an army coach. A bachelor, he had two brothers, one a colonel, the other a station-master in the West of England. He is presumed to have been killed in his fight with Sherlock Holmes at the Reichenbach Falls, near Meiringen, Switzerland. "He is extremely tall and thin, his forehead domes out in a white curve, and his two eyes are deeply sunken in his head. He is clean-shaven, pale, and ascetic-looking, retaining something of the professor in his features. His shoulders are rounded from much study, and his face protrudes forward, and is for ever slowly oscillating from side to side in a curiously reptilian fashion."—Holmes, *The Final Problem.*

MORRIS, BROTHER. A well-disposed and moderate member of the Scowrers of Pennsylvania who pointed out to the brotherhood the dangers of driving small traders out of business. "I tell you, brethren, that our hand is too heavy in this valley."—*The Valley of Fear.*

MORSTAN, MARY. The first Mrs. John H. Watson. The daughter of the late Captain Arthur Morstan,

Professor Moriarty

34th Bombay Infantry, who disappeared on December 3rd, 1878, shortly after arriving in London on twelve months' home leave. Her mother died while she was a child and she was sent home from India to live in an Edinburgh boarding establishment until she was seventeen. In 1882 she was engaged as governess by Mrs. Cecil Forrester, of Lower Camberwell, with whom she remained until her marriage with Watson after the case of *The Sign of Four*, concerning her late father. She died early in the 1890s. 'My mind ran upon our late visitor—her smiles, the deep, rich tones of her voice, the strange mystery which overhung her life. If she were seventeen at the time of her father's disappearance she must be seven-and-twenty now—a sweet age, when youth has lost its self-consciousness and become a little sobered by experience. So I sat and mused, until such dangerous thoughts came into my head that I hurried away to my desk and plunged furiously into the latest treatise upon pathology.'—Watson, *The Sign of Four*. "I think she is one of the most charming young ladies I ever met, and might have been most useful in such work as we have been doing. She had a decided genius that way."—Holmes, *The Sign of Four*.

MORTIMER, JAMES, M.R.C.S. House-surgeon at Charing Cross Hospital, 1882–4. Winner of the Jackson Prize for Comparative Philosophy, with the essay 'Is Disease a Reversion?' Corresponding member of the Swedish Pathological Society. Author of 'Some Freaks of Atavism' (*Lancet*, 1882), 'Do We Progress?' (*Journal of Psychology*, March, 1883). Married in 1884 and set up house at Grimpen, Dartmoor, Devonshire, becoming Medical Officer for Grimpen, Thursley and High Barrow. Medical attendant and personal friend to Sir Charles Baskerville, whose mysterious death he brought to Sherlock Holmes's notice. "You interest me very much, Mr. Holmes. . . . A cast of your skull, sir, until the original is available, would be an ornament to any anthropological museum."—*The Hound of the Baskervilles*.

MOULTON, FRANCIS HAY. Sometime gold prospector and lawful husband of Hatty Doran, the Californian heiress, "I call him a gentleman by courtesy, but he was quite a common-looking person."—Lord St. Simon, *The Noble Bachelor*.

MOUNT-JAMES, LORD. One of the richest men in England. Uncle of Godfrey Staunton, the Rugby International. 'He was dressed in rusty black . . . the whole effect being that of a very rustic parson or of an undertaker's mute.'—Watson. "The old boy is nearly eighty —cram full of gout, too. They say he could chalk his billiard-cue with his knuckles."—Cyril Overton, *The Missing Three-quarter*.

MUNRO, GRANT ('Jack'). Hop merchant, of Norbury, Surrey. Married Effie, widow of John Hebron, of Atlanta, New Jersey, whose inexplicable behaviour caused him to bring to Holmes's attention the case of *The Yellow Face*. "Pipes are occasionally of extraordinary interest. . . . The owner is obviously a muscular man, left-handed, with an excellent set of teeth, careless in his habits, and with no need to practise economy."—Holmes.

MURDOCH, IAN. Mathematical coach at The Gables coaching establishment near Fulworth, Sussex. 'He seemed to live in some high, abstract region of surds and conic sections with little to connect him with ordinary life.'—Holmes, *The Lion's Mane*.

MURILLO, DON JUAN. Deposed Central American dictator living incognito near Oxshott, Surrey. *See* HENDERSON.—*Wisteria Lodge*.

MUSGRAVE, REGINALD, M.P., of Hurlstone Manor, West Sussex. Member of the cadet branch of one of the oldest families in the kingdom, and fellow-student of

Holmes at university. "I never looked at his pale, keen face . . . without associating him with grey archways and mullioned windows and all the venerable wreckage of a feudal keep."—Holmes, *The Musgrave Ritual*.

NELIGAN, JOHN HOPLEY. Son of a partner in the former West Country banking firm of Dawson & Neligan. Suspected by the police of the murder of Captain Peter Carey. "Do you imagine that this anaemic youth was capable of so frightful an assault?"—Holmes, *Black Peter*.

NORBERTON, SIR ROBERT, of Shoscombe Old Place, near Crendall, Berkshire. Gentleman jockey (second in the Derby), boxer, athlete and horse breeder—owner of the Derby winner, Shoscombe Prince. 'He is one of those men who have overshot their true generation. He should have been a buck in the days of the Regency—a boxer, an athlete, a plunger on the Turf, a lover of fair ladies, and, by all account, so far down Queer Street that he may never find his way back again.'—Watson, *Shoscombe Old Place*.

OBERSTEIN, HUGO, alias 'Pierrot'. Foreign agent operating in London during the 1890s from 13, Caulfield Gardens, Kensington. Arrested in the Charing Cross Hotel on his return from Paris in November, 1895, and subsequently sentenced to fifteen years' imprisonment. "There are numerous small fry, but few who would handle so big an affair."—Mycroft Holmes, *The Bruce-Partington Plans*.

OLDACRE, JONAS, alias 'Cornelius', of Deep Dene House, Lower Norwood, Surrey. Prosperous builder of many years' standing. Bachelor, and former fiancé of John Hector McFarlane's mother. "He was more like a malignant and cunning ape than a human being; and he always was, ever since he was a young man."—Mrs. McFarlane, *The Norwood Builder*.

OPENSHAW, JOHN, of Horsham, Sussex. Born 1866, son of Joseph Openshaw of Coventry, patentee of the Openshaw unbreakable bicycle tire, and nephew of Elias Openshaw, a recipient through the post of five mysterious orange pips. Drowned near Waterloo Bridge in 1887. "Young Openshaw shall not remain long unavenged."—Holmes, *The Five Orange Pips*.

ORMSTEIN, WILHELM GOTTSREICH SIGISMOND VON, Grand Duke of Cassel-Falstein and hereditary King of Bohemia. Betrothed to Clotilde Lothman von Saxe-Meningen, second daughter of the King of Scandinavia. Formerly a close friend of Irene Adler. Known at his London hotel (The Langham) as Count von Kramm. 'His dress was rich with a richness which would, in England, be looked upon as akin to bad taste.'—Watson, *A Scandal in Bohemia*.

OVERTON, CYRIL, of Trinity College, Cambridge. Captain of Cambridge University Rugby Football

The King of Bohemia

XV. 'Sixteen stone of solid bone and muscle.'—Watson, *The Missing Three-quarter.*

PARR, LUCY. Second waiting-maid to Alexander Holder and family at Fairbank, Streatham, and a suspect—with her one-legged sweetheart—of the theft of the famous Beryl Coronet. "She is a very pretty girl, and has attracted admirers who have occasionally hung about the place."— Holder, *The Beryl Coronet.*

PETERSON. A London commissionaire, finder of the hat and goose in *The Blue Carbuncle.* "A very honest fellow." —Holmes.

PHELPS, PERCY ('Tadpole'). Civil Servant, of Briar- brae, Woking. Nephew of Lord Holdhurst and school- friend of Watson. His health was much impaired following the theft from his desk in the Foreign Office of a secret treaty for naval co-operation between England and Italy. 'He was, I remember, extremely well connected, and even when we were all little boys together we knew that his mother's brother was Lord Holdhurst, the great Conservative politician. This gaudy re- lationship did him little good at school.'—Watson, *The Naval Treaty.*

'PINNER, ARTHUR AND HARRY.' London agent and managing director respect- ively of the Franco-Midland Hardware Co. (U.K. office, 126B, Corporation Street, Birmingham). *See* BEDD-

Arthur & Harry Pinner

INGTON. "Of course, you expect two brothers to be alike, but not that they should have the same tooth stuffed in the same way."—Hall Pycroft, *The Stockbroker's Clerk*.

PORLOCK, FRED. *Nom de plume* of an informer employed occasionally by Holmes. His message in code brought Holmes the first intimation of the remarkable events at Birlstone, Sussex. "Porlock is important, not for himself, but for the great man with whom he is in touch. Picture to yourself the pilot-fish with the shark, the jackal with the lion— anything that is insignificant in companionship with what is formidable."— Holmes, *The Valley of Fear*.

PRENDERGAST, JACK. Transported to Australia for fraud in 1855, but lost with the convict barque *Gloria Scott*, in which he had led a mutiny. "Now, you don't think it likely that a man who could do anything is going to wear his breeches out sitting in the stinking hold of a rat-gutted, beetle-ridden, mouldy old coffin of a China coaster?"—Prendergast, *The 'Gloria Scott'*.

Jack Prendergast

PRESBURY, PROFESSOR. Eminent physiologist, of Camford University. Born 1842. A widower, with one daughter, he became engaged in 1903 to Alice, daughter of Prof. Morphy, Professor of Comparative Anatomy at Camford. 'A portly, large-featured man, grave, tall, and frock-coated, with the dignity of bearing which a lecturer needs.'—Watson, *The Creeping Man*.

PRESBURY, EDITH. Prof. Presbury's daughter, engaged to her father's assistant, Trevor Bennett. 'A bright, handsome girl of a conventional English type.'—Watson, *The Creeping Man*.

PYCROFT, HALL. Stockbroker's clerk, formerly with Coxon & Woodhouse, Drapers' Gardens. Business manager-elect of the Franco-Midland Hardware Co. 'A smart young City man, of the class who have been labelled Cockneys, but who give us our crack Volunteer regiments, and who turn out more fine athletes and sportsmen than any body of men in these islands.'—Watson, *The Stockbroker's Clerk*.

Hall Pycroft

RANCE, JOHN. Police constable, of 46, Audley Court, Kennington Park Gate, who noticed a light in an empty house (3, Lauriston Gardens, off the Brixton Road) and, upon investigation, discovered the murdered body of Enoch J. Drebber. "I am afraid, Rance, that you will never rise in the force. That head of yours should be for use, as well as ornament."—Holmes, *A Study in Scarlet*.

RAS, DAULAT. Indian student at St. Luke's College. "A quiet, inscrutable fellow . . . well up in his work, though his Greek is his weak subject."—Hilton Soames, *The Three Students*.

RONDER, EUGENIA. Former circus artiste. Widow of Ronder, the showman (Ronder's Wild Beasts) who met his death at Abbas Parva, Berkshire, in circumstances implicating a North African lion, Sahara King. 'From keeping beasts in a cage, the woman seemed, by some retribution of Fate, to have become herself a beast in a cage.'—Watson, *The Veiled Lodger*.

ROSS, COLONEL. Owner of the King's Pyland training stable, near Tavistock, Devonshire, from which his famous racehorse, Silver Blaze, was stolen on the eve of the Wessex Cup race. "The colonel's manner has been just a trifle cavalier to me."—Holmes, *Silver Blaze*.

'ROSS, DUNCAN.' Founder of the Red-Headed League with headquarters at 7, Pope's Court, Fleet Street, administrator of its funds, and employer on the League's behalf of Jabez Wilson. "We have twice been deceived by wigs and once by paint. I could tell you tales of cobbler's wax which would disgust you with human nature."— Ross, *The Red-headed League*.

ROUNDHAY, REV., vicar of Tredannick Wollas, Cornwall, in whose vicarage Mortimer Tregennis, brother of the victims of the 'Cornish Horror', lodged. Bachelor and archaeologist. 'A middle-aged man, portly and affable, with a considerable fund of local lore.'—Watson, *The Devil's Foot*.

ROYLOTT, DR. GRIMESBY. Last survivor of the Roylotts, of Stoke Moran, Surrey, one of the oldest Saxon

families in England. After
his family's fortunes had
declined he took a medical
degree and practised in
Calcutta. Served a long
term of imprisonment after
beating his native butler to
death in a fit of anger, and
later returned to England
with his wife and twin
stepdaughters. His wife
was killed in a railway accident near Crewe. "Violence
of temper approaching to
mania has been hereditary
in the men of the family,
and in my stepfather's case
it had, I believe, been in-
tensified by his long residence in the tropics. . . .
Last week he hurled the
local blacksmith over a
parapet into a stream."—
Helen Stoner, *The Speckled
Band.*

Dr. Grimesby Roylott

RUCASTLE, JEPHRO, of
The Copper Beeches, near
Winchester. Employer of Violet Hunter as governess.
Father of two—a daughter, Alice, by his first wife, and
a son by his second: "One dear little romper, just six
years old. Oh, if you could see him killing cockroaches
with a slipper!"—Rucastle, *The Copper Beeches.*

RYDER, JAMES. Head attendant at the Hotel Cosmo-
politan at the time of the theft of the Countess of Morcar's

priceless carbuncle. 'The
little man stood glancing
from one to the other of us
with half-frightened, half-
hopeful eyes, as one who is
not sure whether he is on
the verge of a windfall or of
a catastrophe.'—Watson,
The Blue Carbuncle.

Jephro Rucastle

ST. CLAIR, NEVILLE, of
The Cedars, near Lee, Kent.
The son of a Chesterfield
schoolmaster, he travelled,
acted and then became a
journalist on a London
evening newspaper before
entering business. He failed
to return home from the City one evening in 1889, but
was subsequently believed to have been seen by his wife
at the window of the Bar of Gold opium den in Upper
Swandam Lane, in the dock area. "Mr. St. Clair is now
thirty-seven years of age, is a man of temperate habits, a
good husband, a very affectionate father, and a man who
is popular with all who know him."—Holmes, *The Man
with the Twisted Lip*.

ST. CLAIR, MRS. NEVILLE. Wife of Neville St. Clair;
a brewer's daughter. "This dear little woman."—Holmes.
'A little blonde woman, clad in some sort of *mousseline de
soie*, with a touch of fluffy pink chiffon at her neck and
wrists.'—Watson, *The Man with the Twisted Lip*.

ST. SIMON, LORD ROBERT WALSINGHAM DE
VERE. Born 1846, second son of the Duke of Balmoral.
Former Under-Secretary for the Colonies. Arms: Azure,
three caltrops in chief over a fess sable. Disappointed

bridegroom of Miss Hatty Doran, the American heiress. "He's forty-one years of age, which is mature for marriage."— Holmes, *The Noble Bachelor*.

SALTIRE, LORD ARTHUR. Heir and only legitimate child of the sixth Duke of Holdernesse. Pupil at the Priory School, near Mackleton, Derbyshire, until his sudden disappearance. "Young Lord Saltire, ten years old . . . a charming youth."—Dr. Thorneycroft Huxtable, *The Priory School*.

SANDEFORD, MR., of Reading. Owner of the sixth bust of Napoleon investigated by Holmes and bought by him for £10 in

Lord Robert St. Simon

The Six Napoleons. An 'elderly, red-faced man with grizzled side-whiskers.'—Watson.

SELDEN, 'the Notting Hill murderer'. Sentenced to life imprisonment at Dartmoor for a crime so atrocious that the death penalty had been commuted on the grounds of possible insanity. Escaped in 1889 and went into hiding on Dartmoor, where he was eventually found dead. "From crime to crime he sank lower and lower . . . but to me, sir, he was always the little curly-headed boy that I had nursed and played with."—Mrs. Barrymore, *The Hound of the Baskervilles*.

SHAFTER, ETTIE. Born 1856, daughter of Jacob Shafter, a Swedish-born boarding house keeper of Sheridan Street, Vermissa, U.S.A. Married in Chicago in 1875 to Birdy Edwards, but died some years after in California. 'She was of the Swedish type, blonde and fair-haired, with the piquant contrast of a pair of beautiful dark eyes.'—*The Valley of Fear*.

SHLESSINGER, REV. DR. Alias of Henry ("Holy") Peters, Australian-born confidence trickster, kidnapper, etc. Disfigured by a bite sustained in a saloon brawl at Adelaide in 1889. Associated with Annie Fraser, a woman masquerading as his wife. "One of the most unscrupulous rascals that Australia has ever evolved—and for a young country it has turned out some very finished types."— Holmes, *The Disappearance of Lady Frances Carfax*.

SHOLTO, BARTHOLOMEW AND THADDEUS. Twin sons of the late Major John Sholto, formerly of the 34th Bombay Infantry, who died April 28th, 1882. Bartholomew was found murdered by poison in his home, Pondicherry Lodge, Upper Norwood, in 1888. "I am a man of somewhat retiring, and I might even say refined, tastes, and there is nothing more unaesthetic than a policeman. I have a natural shrinking from all forms of rough materialism." —Thaddeus Sholto, *The Sign of Four*.

SIMPSON, FITZROY. Amateur bookmaker; a man of excellent birth and education who had squandered a fortune on the turf. Arrested on suspicion of kidnapping Silver Blaze, favourite for the Wessex Cup (at 3 to 1), and murdering his trainer. "An examination of his betting-book shows that bets to the amount of five thousand pounds had been registered by him against the favourite." —Holmes, *Silver Blaze*.

SLANEY, ABE. Former fiancé of Elsie Cubitt while a member of her father's gang in Chicago. 'He was a tall, handsome, swarthy fellow . . . with a panama hat, a bristling black beard, and a great aggressive hooked nose.' —Watson, *The Dancing Men*.

SMALL, JONATHAN. A native of Worcestershire, he enlisted in his late teens in the 3rd Buffs, to escape an amorous entanglement. While serving in India he lost his right leg to a crocodile and was invalided out of the service, becoming labour overseer on an indigo plantation. He escaped massacre by Mutineers and survived the siege of Agra, but was subsequently sentenced to death for being concerned with three Indians in the murder of a wealthy merchant. The sentence was commuted to life imprisonment in the Andaman Islands, from where he escaped by canoe with a native and eventually made his way to London. Arrested by Athelney Jones for his part in the murder of Bartholomew Sholto. "It does seem a queer thing that I, who have a fair claim to half a million of money, should spend the first half of my life building a breakwater in the Andamans, and am like to spend the other half digging drains at Dartmoor." *The Sign of Four*.

SMITH, CULVERTON, of 13, Lower Burke Street, Kensington, and Sumatra. Planter and expert on tropical diseases. Uncle of Victor Savage, who died of an obscure tropical disease, apparently contracted in the heart of London. Called in by Holmes to attempt to cure him of a fatal complaint, caught from Chinese seamen at Rotherhithe. "I don't see you in the witness-box. Quite another shaped box, my good Holmes, I assure you."— Smith, *The Dying Detective*.

SMITH, MORDECAI. Boat proprietor (Smith's Wharf, opposite Millbank). Owner of the steam launch *Aurora*, concerned in the great Thames pursuit of the Agra Treasure. "As long as he has liquor and good pay, why should he ask questions?"—Holmes, *A Study in Scarlet*.

SMITH, WILLOUGHBY. Secretary to Professor Coram at Yoxley Old Place, near Chatham, Kent. Educated at Uppingham and Cambridge. "A decent, quiet, hard-working fellow, with no weak spot in him at all. And yet this is the lad who has met his death this morning in the professor's study under circumstances which can point only to murder."—Stanley Hopkins, *The Golden Pince-nez*.

SMITH, VIOLET. The solitary cyclist of Charlington. Daughter of the late James Smith, conductor of the Imperial Theatre Orchestra. Music teacher to the daughter of Mr. Carruthers, of Chiltern Grange, Surrey, a supposed friend of her late uncle Ralph, recently dead in Johannesburg. She married Cyril Morton, of the Midland Electric Co., Coventry, subsequently senior partner of Morton & Kennedy, electricians, of Westminster. "There is a spirituality about the face . . . which the typewriter does not generate. This lady is a musician."—Holmes, *The Solitary Cyclist*.

SOAMES, HILTON. Tutor and lecturer at the College of St. Luke's 'in one of our great University towns', who consulted Holmes on the problem of *The Three Students*. 'I had always known him to be restless in his manner, but on this particular occasion he was in such a state of uncontrollable agitation that it was clear something very unusual had occurred.'—Watson.

'SPAULDING, VINCENT.' Alias of John Clay, murderer, thief, smasher and forger. Grandson of a royal duke, and ex-scholar of Eton and Oxford. "He'll crack a crib in Scotland one week, and be raising money to build an orphanage in Cornwall the next."—Peter Jones, *The Red-headed League.*

STACKHURST, HAROLD. Scholar and university Blue (rowing). Proprietor of The Gables scholastic coaching establishment, near Fulworth, Sussex. 'He and I were always friendly from the day I came to the coast, and he was the one man who was on such terms with me that we could drop in on each other in the evenings without an invitation.'—Holmes, *The Lion's Mane.*

STAMFORD. A dresser at St. Bartholomew's Hospital who worked under Watson during his studies there. A chance reunion with him at the Criterion Bar resulted in his introducing Watson to Sherlock Holmes. 'The sight of a friendly face in the great wilderness of London is a pleasant thing indeed to a lonely man. In old days Stamford had never been a particular crony of mine, but now I hailed him with enthusiasm.'—Watson. *A Study in Scarlet.*

STANGERSON, JOSEPH. Formerly of Salt Lake City, Utah. Principal Elder of the Church of Latter Day Saints, and private secretary to Enoch J. Drebber. Found murdered at Halliday's Private Hotel, Little George Street, London. "He was cunning, was Stangerson, and always on his guard."—Jefferson Hope, *A Study in Scarlet.*

STAPLETON, JOHN AND BERYL, of Merripit House, Dartmoor, Devonshire, and neighbours of the Baskerville family. John, a keen naturalist, discovered the Vandaleur Moth. "His grey clothes and jerky, zigzag, irregular progress made him not unlike some huge moth himself."—Watson. He was formerly headmaster of St. Oliver's private school, York. It was Beryl Stapleton who issued a warning to Sir Henry Baskerville to leave Dartmoor and return to London. 'There is something tropical and exotic about her which forms a singular contrast to her cool and unemotional brother.' — Watson, *The Hound of the Baskervilles*.

STARK, COLONEL LYSANDER ('Fritz'). Murderer and counterfeiter, of Eyford, Berkshire. "A man rather over the middle size but of an exceeding thinness. I do not think that I have ever seen so thin a man."—Victor Hatherley, *The Engineer's Thumb*.

STAUNTON, GODFREY. The missing three-quarter of the Cambridge University Rugby XV. Represented England (five times) and Blackheath. Nephew and heir of Lord Mount-James. "Whether it's passing, or tackling, or dribbling, there's no one to touch him."—Cyril Overton, *The Missing Three-quarter*.

Beryl Stapleton

STEILER, PETER (THE ELDER). Landlord of the Englischer Hof, Meiringen, Switzerland, where Holmes and Watson stayed the night before the Reichenbach

incident. Had been a waiter
for three years at the
Grosvenor Hotel, London.
The Final Problem.

STERNDALE, DR. LEON.
Famous lion-hunter and explorer, of Africa and Beau-
champ Arriance, Cornwall.
Married, but separated
from his wife. A distant
cousin of the Tregennis
family. "I have lived so
long among savages and
beyond the law that I have
got into the way of being a
law unto myself."—Stern-
dale, *The Devil's Foot.*

STOCKDALE, BARNEY.
Husband of Susan, maid to
Mrs. Mary Maberley, of
The Three Gables, Harrow
Weald. Member of the
Spencer John gang, and employer of Steve Dixie. "They
specialise in assaults, intimidation, and the like."—
Holmes, *The Three Gables.*

Colonel Lysander Stark

STONER, HELEN, of Manor Stoke House, near Leather-
head, Surrey. Born 1853, daughter of Major-General
Stoner, Bengal Artillery, twin sister of the late Julia
Stoner, and stepdaughter of Dr. Grimesby Roylott.
Engaged to Percy, second son of Mr. Armitage, of Crane
Water, near Reading. "I have no one to turn to—none,

Helen Stoner

Silver Blaze

save only one, who cares for me, and he, poor fellow, can be of little aid."—Helen Stoner, *The Speckled Band*.

STRAKER, JOHN. Alias William Darbyshire. Retired jockey; trainer at Colonel Ross's stable, King's Pyland, near Tavistock, Devonshire. Believed to have been murdered trying to prevent the kidnapping of the famous racehorse, Silver Blaze. "I have always found him an excellent servant."— Colonel Ross. "As a man of the world, Colonel, you know that men do not carry other people's bills about in their pockets."— Holmes, *Silver Blaze*.

SUTHERLAND, MARY, of 31, Lyon Place, Camberwell. Daughter of a plumber in Tottenham Court Road; step-daughter of James Windibank, and fiancée of Hosmer Angel. Heiress to her Uncle Ned, of Auckland, New Zealand. 'A large woman with a heavy fur boa round her neck, and a large curling red feather in a broad-brimmed hat which was tilted in a coquettish Duchess-of-Devonshire fashion over her ear.'—Watson, *A Case of Identity*.

Mary Sutherland

SYLVIUS, COUNT NEGRETTO, of 136, Moorside Gardens, London, N.W. Big-game hunter, sportsman, card-player and man-about-town. Concerned in a number of cases not documented by Watson, including the 1892 Riviera train-robbery, the Crédit Lyonnais cheque forgery, and the cases of Mrs. Harold and Miss Minnie Warrender. "Possibly you have heard of his reputation as a shooter of big game. It would indeed be a triumphant ending to his excellent sporting record if he added me to his bag."—Holmes, *The Mazarin Stone*.

TONGA. A native of the Andaman Islands who befriended the convict, Jonathan Small, and enabled him to escape from the penal settlement in his canoe. He shared Small's subsequent travels, allowing himself to be exhibited as 'the black cannibal' at fairgrounds in England. Lost his life during the pursuit of the Agra Treasure. 'Somewhere in the dark ooze at the bottom of the Thames lie the bones of that strange visitor to our shores.'—Watson, *The Sign of Four*.

TREGENNIS, BRENDA, of Tredannick Wartha, Cornwall. Sister of Mortimer, George and Owen Tregennis. 'Her dark, clear-cut face was handsome, even in death.'—Watson, *The Devil's Foot*.

TREGENNIS, GEORGE AND OWEN, of Tredannick Wartha, Cornwall. Retired from a tin-mining concern at Redruth to live in seclusion with their sister Brenda. Victims of 'The Cornish Horror'. "George and Owen were singing snatches of song and gibbering like two great apes."—Mortimer Tregennis, *The Devil's Foot*.

TREGENNIS, MORTIMER, of the Vicarage, Tredannick Wollas, near Tredannick Wartha, Cornwall. Brother of Brenda, George and Owen Tregennis. "A sly, subtle, scheming man."—Dr. Leon Sterndale, *The Devil's Foot*.

TREVELYAN, DR. PERCY. Doctor of Medicine; graduate of London University; winner of the Bruce Pinkerton prize and medal for his monograph on obscure nervous lesions. He was enabled to give up a minor position at King's College Hospital and commence private practice at 403, Brook Street, through the patronage of a Mr. Blessington. 'His age may not have been more than three or four and thirty, but his haggard expression and unhealthy hue told of a life which had sapped his strength and robbed him of his youth.'—Watson, *The Resident Patient*.

'TREVOR', JAMES. Justice of the Peace, of Donnithorpe, near Langmere, Norfolk. Formerly James Armitage, employed by a London banking house. At the age of twenty-two he had been convicted of embezzlement and sentenced to transportation to Australia. He was one of the few survivors of the convict transport *Gloria Scott*, which disappeared with the loss of almost all her hundred convicts and crew during a passage from Falmouth in 1855. He subsequently became a gold-miner and pugilist, before returning to England. "He was a man of little culture, but with a considerable amount of rude strength both physically and mentally."—Holmes, *The 'Gloria Scott'*.

TREVOR, VICTOR. Tea planter, son of James Trevor, J.P. A former college friend of Holmes. "He was the only friend I made during the two years that I was at college . . . and that only through the accident of his bull-terrier freezing on to my ankle one morning as I went down to chapel."—Holmes, *The 'Gloria Scott'*.

TURNER, JOHN. Landowner, of Boscombe Valley, near Ross-on-Wye, Herefordshire. He made his money in Australia, where he became acquainted with Charles

McCarthy, subsequently the tenant of one of his farms. Widower and father of Alice Turner. 'His tangled beard, grizzled hair, and outstanding, drooping eyebrows combined to give an air of dignity and power to his appearance.'—Watson. "Black Jack of Ballarat was the name I went under."—Turner, *The Boscombe Valley Mystery*.

TURNER, ALICE. Only daughter of John Turner and friend since childhood of James, the son of Charles McCarthy. "I cannot admire his taste if it is indeed a fact that he was averse to a marriage with so charming a young lady as this Miss Turner."—Watson, *The Boscombe Valley Mystery*.

VON BORK. German secret agent before World War I, chosen by the Kaiser for a special mission because of his remarkable talents for espionage. "The most astute secret service man in Europe."—Baron Von Herling. "He was in a class by himself."—Holmes, *His Last Bow*.

John Turner

Von Herling, Baron. Chief Secretary of the German Legation in London in 1914. "The heavens, too, may not be quite so peaceful if all that the good Zeppelin promises us comes true."—Von Herling, *His Last Bow*.

Walter, Sir James. Head of the Submarine Department at Woolwich Arsenal at the time of the theft, in 1895, of the Bruce-Partington plans, for whose security he was responsible. He died within a few days of the occurrence. "My brother, Sir James, was a man of very sensitive honour, and he could not survive such an affair." —Colonel Valentine Walter, *The Bruce-Partington Plans*.

Walter, Colonel Valentine. Born 1845, younger brother of Sir James Walter. Arrested at 13, Caulfield Gardens, Kensington, in November, 1895. "As to murder, I am as innocent as you."—Colonel Walter, *The Bruce-Partington Plans*.

Warren, Mrs., of Great Orme Street, London, W.C. Wife of a timekeeper at Morton & Wainwright's, Tottenham Court Road. Holmes twice had occasion to act in connection with lodgers of hers. 'The landlady had the pertinacity, and also the cunning, of her sex.'—Watson, *The Red Circle*.

West, Arthur Cadogan. A clerk at Woolwich Arsenal, he was found dead in November, 1895, at the age of twenty-seven, beside a railway line just outside Aldgate Underground station, having apparently fallen from a train. Secret documents of national importance were found in his pockets. "Arthur was the most single-minded, chivalrous, patriotic man upon earth."—Violet Westbury, *The Bruce-Partington Plans*.

Westbury, Violet. Fiancée of Arthur Cadogan West. He had left her abruptly, on their way to a theatre, a few hours before his body was found beside the Underground railway line. "The call must have been very pressing, since he left his girl standing in the fog."—Holmes, *The Bruce-Partington Plans.*

WHITNEY, ISA. A patient of Watson's and husband of an old school friend of the first Mrs. Watson. Brother of the late Elias Whitney, D.D., Principal of the Theological College of St. George's. 'Having read De Quincey's description of his dreams and sensations, he had drenched his tobacco in laudanum in an attempt to produce the same effects. He found, as so many more have done, that the practice is easier to attain than to get rid of.'—Watson, *The Man with the Twisted Lip.*

WIGGINS. An urchin, of no fixed abode; leader of the Baker Street Irregulars. 'The spokesman of the street arabs, young Wiggins, introduced his insignificant and unsavoury person.'—Watson, *A Study in Scarlet.*

WILDER, JAMES. Natural son of, and secretary to, the sixth Duke of Holdernesse; half-brother to Lord Saltire. "When I was a young man, Mr. Holmes, I loved with such a love as comes only once in a lifetime. . . . She died and left this one child, whom for her sake I have cherished and cared for."— Holdernesse, *The Priory School.*

James Wilder

WILLIAMSON. Tenant of Charlington Hall, near Farnham, Surrey, where he lived alone with a small staff of servants. "There is some rumour that he is or has been a clergyman: but one or two incidents of his short residence at the Hall struck me as peculiarly unecclesiastical."—Holmes, *The Solitary Cyclist.*

WILSON, JABEZ, of Coburg Square. Widower and pawn-broker with a declining business, he was introduced by his assistant, Vincent Spaulding, to the Red-Headed League. 'Bore every mark of being an average commonplace British tradesman, obese, pompous and slow. There was nothing remarkable about the man save his blazing red head.'—Watson, *The Red-headed League.*

Jabez Wilson

WINDIBANK, JAMES, of 31, Lyon Place, Camberwell. Stepfather of Mary Sutherland. Traveller for Westhouse & Marbank, claret importers, of Fenchurch Street. "He would get mad if I wanted so much as to join a Sunday-school treat."—Mary Sutherland, *A Case of Identity.*

WINDIGATE. Landlord of the Alpha Inn, near the British Museum. 'The ruddy, white-aproned landlord.'—Watson, *The Blue Carbuncle.*

WINTER, KITTY. A victim of Baron Adelbert Gruner, enlisted by Shinwell Johnson to assist Holmes in the rescue from matrimony of Violet de Merville. 'A slim. flame-like young woman with a pale, intense face, youthful, and yet so worn with sin and sorrow that one read the terrible years which had left their leprous mark upon her.'—Watson, *The Illustrious Client.*

WOOD, HENRY. Former corporal in the Royal Mallows (formerly 117th Foot). Captured by rebels during the Indian Mutiny and subsequently enslaved in North India. Lived as a wandering conjurer in Afghanistan and the Punjab before returning to England in his old age. "You see me now with my back like a camel and my ribs all awry, but there was a time when Corporal Henry Wood was the smartest man in the 117th Foot."—*The Crooked Man*.

Henry Wood

WOODLEY, JOHN. Friend and associate of Robert Carruthers, of Chiltern Grange, Farnham, Surrey, where he annoyed Violet Smith, the music teacher, with his attentions. "Mr. Woodley seemed to me to be a most odious person. He was for ever making eyes at me."—Miss Smith. "Do you tell me that that girl, that angel, is to be tied to Roaring Jack Woodley for life?"—Carruthers, *The Solitary Cyclist*.

WRIGHT, THERESA. Maid to Lady Brackenstall at the Abbey Grange, Marsham, Kent, and her nurse in her infancy. Born in Australia. "The kind of maid you don't pick up nowadays."—Stanley Hopkins, *The Abbey Grange*.

PLOTS OF THE STORIES

INDEX TO PLOTS

(With dates of first publication in book form)

A STUDY IN SCARLET.   John H. Watson, M.D., late of the Army Medical Department, returns to London with wounds incurred in the second Afghan War and a pension of 11s. 6d. a day. He is homeless and friendless. He tells his troubles in the Criterion Bar to young Stamford, once his dresser at Bart's, and, as it happens, just the man to help him. He knows a man who has just taken rooms in Baker Street and is looking for someone to share them: that man is Sherlock Holmes.

The two men have not been sharing one another's company and eccentricities for long before Watson learns that Holmes is a consulting detective, helping Scotland Yard in a private capacity. As confirmation, a case at once crops up, and Watson finds himself invited to share the adventure. "A bad business at 3, Lauriston Gardens, off the Brixton Road," is the description applied to it by Inspector Tobias Gregson. An American named Enoch J. Drebber has been murdered, and no clue exists save the word 'Rache', scrawled in blood on the wall. No clue, that is, to Gregson and his colleague Lestrade. Holmes is able to deduce a little more and is less surprised than the police when Stangerson, the dead man's private secretary, is murdered—with 'Rache' again written in blood nearby—*after* the chief suspect has been placed under lock and key.

Where the police and their resources have failed, Holmes and his succeed. Does not one member of the Baker Street Irregulars equal any dozen police? And is not 'Rache' the German for 'Revenge'?

Beeton's Christmas Annual, 1887

THE SIGN OF FOUR.   Sherlock Holmes is weary of inactivity, and turns to his old consolation, cocaine: "My mind rebels at stagnation . . . give me problems, give me work . . . what is the use of having powers, doctor, when one has no field upon which to exert them?'' He has hardly finished speaking when a card is handed in—that of Miss Mary Morstan. She proves to be such a charming young lady that Watson at once loses his susceptible heart. Holmes is only interested in the puzzle she sets him. Mary Morstan is the daughter of Captain Morstan, an Indian Army officer who had disappeared in London ten years before and has not been heard of since. Four years after his strange disappearance, Miss Morstan, now a governess, had received an anonymous gift of a very large and lustrous pearl, since when she has received a pearl each year, with still no clue to the sender. But on the day of her visit to Holmes a summons has reached her to meet the unknown giver outside the Lyceum Theatre at seven that evening. 'If you are distrustful, bring two friends. You are a wronged woman, and shall have justice.' Holmes and Watson agree to accompany her to the rendezvous, and Holmes meanwhile does a little research, which shows that Major Sholto, the vanished Captain Morstan's only friend in London, had died within a week of Miss Morstan's receiving the first pearl.

The rendezvous is kept, and the three are taken by an uncommunicative coachman to the strange abode of Mr. Thaddeus Sholto—'an oasis of art in the howling desert of South London'. This eccentric hypochondriac proves to be the son of the late Major Sholto, and twin-brother of Bartholomew Sholto of Pondicherry Lodge, Upper Norwood. On his death-bed, Major Sholto had told his two sons of the wonderful Agra Treasure, to which Miss Morstan is rightful heir, her father having died of apoplexy when arguing with Major Sholto about its disposal. Holmes, Watson, and Miss Morstan accompany Thaddeus to Pondicherry Lodge to reclaim the treasure, but arrive to find brother Bartholomew dead from poisoning, and the treasure gone. A trail of footsteps leads Holmes and Watson on a thrilling chase after the murderer, following which they hear the strange story of Jonathan Small, Tonga, the faithful Andaman Islander, and the Agra Treasure, for whose possession several men have died.

Lippincott's Monthly Magazine
(England & U.S.A.), 1890

A SCANDAL IN BOHEMIA.   The King of Bohemia has chosen the wrong woman for an indiscreet liaison. Irene Adler, 'with the face of the most beautiful of women and the mind of the most resolute of men', is not one to be discarded lightly, and the King's marriage with the second daughter of the Scandinavian monarch is unlikely to pass without prior incident. Only three days are left before the nuptials, and His Majesty does well to engage Sherlock Holmes to make one last attempt to obtain possession of a certain photograph before Irene can forward it to the bride's royal parents.

Holmes will need all his ingenuity. Five attempts have already been made by others without success, and a woman of Irene's character will clearly be no mean adversary. But Holmes has his resources, too, including the ability to impersonate a drunken-looking groom and an amiable and simple-minded Nonconformist clergyman; and he has—for so avowed a misogynist—a pretty insight into female psychology.

The Strand Magazine, 1891

THE RED-HEADED LEAGUE.   With his pawnbroking business at a slack period, Jabez Wilson is doubly delighted to discover that he has been carrying about a considerable financial asset without knowing it. It would never have occurred to him that his head of fine red hair and a mere four hours a day of his time could be worth £4 a week, had Fate not sent him a new assistant, Vincent Spaulding, with a sharp eye for the classified advertisement columns. From a queue of red-heads which choked Fleet Street and included 'straw, lemon, orange, brick, Irish-setter, liver, clay', he is pleasantly surprised to be singled out as Mr. Duncan Ross's choice.

The work is not very edifying: copying out the *Encyclopaedia Britannica*. But the appointment is virtually a sinecure, an eccentric American millionaire's way of expressing sympathy for fellow red-heads and doing a good turn to his old home town. So well, in fact, does it suit the pawnbroker that when it comes abruptly to an end he is moved to consult Sherlock Holmes, whose solution to this 'three-pipe problem' is a nocturnal visit to the cellar of a London bank.

The Strand Magazine, 1891

A CASE OF IDENTITY. To Watson's surprise, the rambling and seemingly inconsequential narrative of Miss Mary Sutherland, the large woman in the large hat with a large feather, provokes no signs of impatience in Holmes. The anxiety of a late plumber's daughter over Mr. Hosmer Angel, her vanished bridegroom-to-be ("I met him at the gas-fitters' ball") would seem to offer little real interest. The circumstances of her plight are not even new to Holmes: at least two parallels lie in his indexes. It is 'the maiden herself', rather than her problem, who interests Holmes; together with the importance of sleeves, the suggestiveness of thumbnails, and the thought that great issues may hang from a bootlace. An interview with Mr. James Windibank, her stepfather, is sufficient to clear up every detail but one; and it is not going to be Holmes who will attend to that. He is too mindful of the old Persian saying: 'There is danger for him who taketh the tiger cub and danger also for whoso snatches a delusion from a woman'.

The Strand Magazine, 1891

THE BOSCOMBE VALLEY MYSTERY. Watson's experience of camp life in Afghanistan has left him a prompt

'They found the body'
The Boscombe Valley Mystery

and ready traveller, whose wants are few and simple, and he is able easily to cope with a breakfast-table summons to join Holmes on the platform at Paddington in ample time to board the 11.15 to the West Country. The case they are to investigate is apparently a simple one, and therefore not so: 'The more featureless and commonplace a crime is, the more difficult it is to bring it home', is an aphorism which Holmes has been known to utter more than once.

Two people had seen Charles McCarthy striding from his farmhouse in the direction of Boscombe Pool, and one of them had noticed his son, James McCarthy, follow shortly after him, carrying a gun. A child picking flowers had shortly after seen the two men quarrelling violently, and before much longer had elapsed the younger of them had come flying from the pool—gunless, hatless and blood-stained—with the news of his father's murder by a person unknown. Not surprisingly, he is now the occupant of a cell, awaiting trial at the next Assizes. But Holmes has another observation for Watson to cogitate upon: "There is nothing more deceptive than an obvious fact."

The Strand Magazine, 1891

THE FIVE ORANGE PIPS. Colonel Elias Openshaw was the first to receive, by post from Pondicherry, five orange pips in an envelope with 'K.K.K.' scrawled in red ink on its inner flap. Within a few weeks he was dead, apparently the victim of his own hand. The next recipient of orange pips was his brother Joseph. The letter this time came from less far afield—from Dundee—and Joseph Openshaw's death followed correspondingly quickly.

No wonder, then, that young John Openshaw should hasten to 221B, Baker Street, so late on so wild a night. The envelope addressed to him and enclosing five orange pips has been posted only a matter of miles away; and two precious days have already been allowed to slip away through indecision and official incomprehension. The case is one of the most fantastic to come their way, Holmes assures his colleague and friend. Before much longer it has also become a personal matter; Sherlock Holmes's pride has been hurt.

The Strand Magazine, 1891

THE MAN WITH THE TWISTED LIP. While retrieving Isa Whitney from a lost mid-week in the Bar of Gold opium den near the London docks, Watson encounters Holmes, who bears him off to Kent, to the house of another missing person, Neville St. Clair, a business-man who has not returned home for four days. Mrs. St. Clair tells them of passing the Bar of Gold on the day after her husband's disappearance and momentarily glimpsing his face at the window. The police have found that a window-sill over-looking the river bears traces of blood. Portions of St. Clair's clothing, hidden behind a curtain, and a box of bricks which he had promised to bring home for his little boy, have been found on the same unsavoury premises. The occupant of the room in which these discoveries have been made—Hugh Boone, a sinister cripple, well known as a beggar in the City—is under arrest on suspicion of having murdered the missing man, whose coat has since been found on a river mud-bank, weighted with the con-tents of its pockets: 421 pennies and 70 halfpennies.

The solution to this bizarre mystery, Holmes finds, lies not in the river, but in the St. Clairs' bathroom, a con-clusion which it takes him an ounce of shag tobacco and an all-night sitting on five cushions to reach.

The Strand Magazine, 1891

THE BLUE CARBUNCLE. Calling to wish Holmes belated Christmas greetings, Watson finds him con-templating a disreputable hard felt hat. This, together with a fine, fat goose, has been brought to Holmes by Peterson, a commissionaire, who had picked them up after

'At the foot of the stairs she met this Lascar scoundrel'
The Man with the Twisted Lip

their owner had fled from a street brawl. While Holmes is reading the character of the owner, Henry Baker, from his hat, Peterson returns with a jewel, found by his wife in the crop of the goose, which Holmes had given back to him to eat. Holmes recognizes it as the Countess of Morcar's priceless blue carbuncle, believed to have been stolen from her hotel room by a plumber who had been left alone there to repair the fire-grate. Holmes's and Watson's inquiry takes them to an inn near the British Museum and to the stall of a poultry dealer, in Covent Garden market.

After losing a bet, Holmes can still retain sufficient fellow-feeling to compound a felony at the season of forgiveness.

The Strand Magazine, 1892

THE SPECKLED BAND.   When Miss Julia Stoner cried out to her sister: "O, my God! Helen! it was the band!" her allusion was in no sense orchestral; for she added "The speckled band!" and lapsed into an unconsciousness from which she never recovered. In retailing the incident to Sherlock Holmes, Helen Stoner inclines to the view that a band of gipsies, or even, more specifically, their spotted-handkerchief headgear, might have sprung somehow to her sister's demented mind.

Working as he does rather for the love of his art than for the acquirement of wealth, Holmes only demands of an investigation that it should 'tend towards the unusual, and even the fantastic'; and, certainly, he has no need to stretch this principle to embrace the remarkable occurrences at Stoke Moran. The unusual is present in abundance: whistles in the night, a cheetah and a baboon roaming freely in the grounds, the sudden clang as of a mass of metal falling; and the ever-sinister supervision of the brawling, bullying Dr. Grimesby Roylott, whose name deserves to rank with Palmer's and Pritchard's for

'He made neither sound nor motion'

The Speckled Band

notoriety amongst his profession. Still, if Dr. Roylott can
bend a poker with his bare hands, Holmes can straighten
it again with his; and Watson has his trusty Eley's No. 2
nestling in his pocket to help sustain them through a night
that must bring horrors enough before it is over.

The Strand Magazine, 1892

THE ENGINEER'S THUMB.   Dr. Watson is aroused
early to treat an emergency case, Victor Hatherley, who
might have bled to death following the loss of his thumb,
but for his expert knowledge of hydraulic principles. The
patient's account of his 'accident' has Watson hurrying
him round to repeat it to Holmes.

Hatherley recounts a visit to his office by a Colonel
Lysander Stark, requesting him, for a fee equivalent to

double what he had earned in all of three years, to go at once to his house in Berkshire to repair a hydraulic press used for processing fuller's earth. Secrecy was enjoined: should the colonel's neighbours learn of the presence of this valuable commodity in their district they would refuse to sell him their fuller's-earth-bearing land. Hatherley had accepted the commission, but having examined the press had had no more discretion than to observe that so powerful a machine could scarcely be required for so simple a process. In consequence, he had lost not only his fee, but a thumb.

Given a brief description of a horse, glimpsed by lamplight, and a recollection of tales of pirates, Holmes is not long in supplying an explanation and a word of consolatory advice.

The Strand Magazine, 1892

THE NOBLE BACHELOR. "I had formed my conclusions as to the case before our client came into the room," Holmes is able to tell an astonished Watson. But even a foregone conclusion, and the pompousness of Lord St. Simon, cannot deter him from following up the incident of a nobleman deserted at his wedding reception by his rich American bride, Hatty Doran. The police, too, have drawn their conclusion—that she had been decoyed away by a former recipient of his lordship's condescension, Flora Millar, whose ejection had been an earlier feature of the ill-fated festivities. But Holmes's thoughts are upon the business with the bouquet, the man in the front pew, and a receipt from one of the few London hotels exclusive enough to ask, and get, eight shillings for a bed and half a crown for breakfast.

If, having been provided with a solution, the English aristocrat will not sit down to a celebratory supper, the 'common-looking' American will, moving Holmes to remark: "It is always a joy to me to meet an American,

Mr. Moulton, for I am one of those who believe that the folly of a monarch and the blundering of a Minister in far-gone years will not prevent our children from being someday citizens of the same world-wide community under a flag which shall be the quartering of the Union Jack with the Stars and Stripes.''

The Strand Magazine, 1892

THE BERYL CORONET.   The 'madman' observed by Watson making his eccentric progress towards 221B, Baker Street, turns out to be none other than Alexander Holder, one of London's leading bankers. His agitation seems justified. The priceless Beryl Coronet, a treasure of national importance, has been stolen while in his possession as security against a large loan. The coronet has since been retrieved, albeit with a piece missing: it is the identity of the suspected thief that has brought one of the foremost of citizens to this pitiable pass. Holder had surprised his own son, Arthur, at dead of night, apparently in the act of breaking pieces off the coronet.

At the scene of the crime, Holmes tests his strength and the breaking-point of gold, contemplates the spoor of a one-legged greengrocer, beards a blackguard, and is at length able to deliver Mr. Holder a little homily upon filial relationship.

The Strand Magazine, 1892

THE COPPER BEECHES.   To an out-of-work governess accustomed to a salary of £48 a year, Mr. Jephro Rucastle's offer of £30 a quarter could not have been anything but alluring; save for one detail—the curious conditions he stipulated. Miss Violet Hunter must be prepared to sit where she was told, wear any dress required, and, worst of all, cut short her beautiful chestnut hair. Economic considerations had at length prevailed: after all, there *was* a Mrs. Rucastle, and the commands, if eccentric, were "such as a lady might with propriety obey". But it is as well that Miss Hunter decided to confide her doubts to Sherlock Holmes before leaving to take charge of the sadistic six-year-old heir to 'The Copper Beeches', near Winchester. At the receipt of her urgent telegram, Holmes and Watson are alert to repair at once to her side and determine which of seven explanations covering the known facts is to be proved correct by fresh information awaiting them; information, as it turns out, concerning a dog as large as a calf, a locked room in an unused wing of the house, and an impertinent loiterer with nothing better to do than to gape from the roadway outside while Miss Hunter rocks with laughter at her employer's jokes. "I think, Watson, that it would be as well for you to have your pistol ready," Holmes is moved to remark; and not long passes before it is needed.

The Strand Magazine, 1892

SILVER BLAZE. It comes as no surprise to Watson to be told by Holmes that they must leave London at once for Dartmoor. The extraordinary happenings at the King's Pyland racehorse training stables, near Tavistock, are already the topic of conversation through the length and breadth of England.

Silver Blaze, the most famous racehorse in the country and 3 to 1 favourite for the valuable Wessex Cup, has been kidnapped and his trainer, John Straker, murdered— evidently in an attempt to rescue the animal. Fitzroy Simpson, an amateur bookmaker, is already in custody as the obvious suspect for both crimes and has readily admitted to having loitered near Silver Blaze's stall and engaged his stable boy in conversation on the fatal night, not long before the boy had been found drugged.

But in Holmes's view, the circumstantial evidence against Simpson could be torn to rags by a clever counsel. If he really is the guilty party, other proof must be forth-

'*He laid his hand upon the glossy neck*'

Silver Blaze

coming. A very singular knife, a wax vesta, a lame sheep
and a dog that did nothing in the night-time seem to him
likely to provide a true solution to the case.

The Strand Magazine, 1892

THE YELLOW FACE. Even when Holmes erred, the
truth was still discovered, says Watson at the beginning
of this chronicle of one of his friend's failures.

Holmes and Watson return from a springtime walk in
Regent's Park to find that a client has called in their
absence—"a very restless gentleman". Mr. Grant Munro
reveals that his wife is the cause of his visit. For three
years they have been happily married, but for the past
few days he has sensed that although her love for him is
undiminished, a barrier has sprung up between them.
Effie Munro had been Effie Hebron when he married her
—a widow who had lived in America, where her first
husband was a lawyer. He and their child having died of
yellow fever, she returned to England, with a comfortable
fortune, and met and married Grant Munro. They had
been extremely happy in their semi-rural home at Norbury, until the day when Mrs. Munro demanded a hundred
pounds from him, without explanation. Shortly afterwards,
when passing a cottage near his house, Munro had noted
that it was no longer empty. Speculating on the new
tenants, he saw a strange face at the window, "unnatural
and inhuman". Some days later he met his wife emerging
from this very cottage, and a great suspicion sprang up in
his mind. She refused to dispel it or to explain.

"I am afraid that this is a bad business, Watson,"
says Holmes; but for once his conclusions have very little
to do with the real facts.

The Strand Magazine, 1892

THE STOCKBROKER'S CLERK. After several months'
unemployment, following the failure of the firm which he

had served for five years, Hall Pycroft, a young stock-broker's clerk, has secured a place with one of the best financial houses in the City of London. Before he has time to begin work, however, a far better prospect materializes in the form of an approach by the Franco-Midland Hardware Company's London agent, Arthur Pinner, who, evidently finding Pycroft all he has been recommended to be, has no hesitation in offering him the post of business manager of the company. The appointment is subject to the agreement of Pinner's brother Harry, the promoter and managing director-elect of this new company, but this is readily forthcoming when he interviews Pycroft at the firm's temporary offices in Birmingham.

Pycroft is troubled, though. Instead of proceeding to Paris to take up his duties he has been kept in Birmingham copying out lists of hardware and furniture firms from a directory. And having seen his employer laugh he has made up his mind to consult Sherlock Holmes, who, in discovering why Mr. Pycroft is being so assiduously detained in the provinces, is unfortunately too late to forestall murder in London.

The Strand Magazine, 1893

THE 'GLORIA SCOTT'.   "Rather grotesque than other-wise," is Watson's reaction to the message which had struck Justice of the Peace Trevor dead with horror upon reading it: 'The supply of game for London is going steadily up. Head-keeper Hudson, we believe, has been now told to receive all orders for fly-paper, and for preservation of your hen-pheasant's life.'

The case is a reminiscence of Holmes's student days. Invited to stay with his friend Victor Trevor, the J.P.'s son, he had chanced to be present when a sinister sailorman named Hudson arrived to claim the magistrate as a ship-mate of thirty years before. An older, more experienced Holmes might have recognized then and there the danger concealed behind the sailor's request for hospitality. But though not yet embarked upon his great career, he had not long to wait before receiving an urgent summons to the dying J.P.'s home, to hear a strange tale of mutiny in a convict transport bound for Australia.

The Strand Magazine, 1893

THE MUSGRAVE RITUAL. A crumpled piece of paper, an old-fashioned brass key, a peg of wood with a ball of string attached, and three rusty old discs of metal: this curious collection is all that remains to remind Holmes of one of his earliest cases, the singular—and in many ways unique—business of the Musgrave Ritual.

Like the case of the *Gloria Scott*, this belongs to the days before the joining of forces with Watson and taking up residence in Baker Street. Again, it involves a college acquaintance of Holmes, this time Reginald Musgrave, inheritor of West Sussex estates and the manor house of Hurlstone, perhaps the oldest inhabited building in the country. With these Musgrave has also inherited the services of the family butler, Brunton; services which he has not had long to enjoy. His purpose, in fact, in seeking the advice of young Mr. Sherlock Holmes of Montague Street is to find out what has become of the butler since his sudden disappearance after receiving notice of dismissal for rifling a bureau and reading a document relating to a certain family ceremony—the mysterious Musgrave Ritual. Holmes finds himself on the track not only of a butler, but of treasure.

"Whose was it?"
"His who is gone."
"Who shall have it?"
"He who will come."
What it was, even Holmes is surprised to discover.

The Strand Magazine, 1893

THE REIGATE SQUIRES   Holmes is exhausted. Even his iron constitution had to fail after two months of working not less than fifteen hours a day, to earn the congratulations of all Europe for his handling of the case of Baron Maupertuis and the Netherland-Sumatra Company. Watson seizes the chance to take up an invitation from his old friend of the Afghan campaign, Colonel Hayter, for them both to visit his peaceful bachelor establishment near Reigate, in Surrey.

But the Reigate district is not at its most peaceful. Thieves have just ransacked the library of one of the colonel's neighbouring squires; and within a few hours of Holmes's arrival there comes news of further criminal activity—murder, this time. Watson's professional protestations cannot stop his patient from accepting the investigating police officer's invitation to 'step across' and lend a hand. The strain of accepting is to bring on a fit; and his companions may be forgiven for concluding that Holmes's mental powers are in temporary decline. Yet he remains alert enough to solve, by advanced principles of graphology, the murder of a coachman.

The Strand Magazine, 1893

THE CROOKED MAN. "It is the supposed murder of Colonel Barclay, of the Royal Mallows, at Aldershot, which I am investigating," says Holmes, descending on Watson at his Paddington home one summer evening. The good doctor is just about to retire—his wife has already done so—but the lure of Holmes with a new problem is too much for him.

Colonel Barclay, attached to the Royal Mallows, had lived out of barracks in married quarters, in a detached house called Lachine. A man of uncertain temper and violent moods, he had never been known to turn this side of his nature on his wife, to whom he was devoted. Yet an altercation between them had been heard just before a loud cry from the colonel had brought his coachman to the morning-room, to find his master stone dead in a pool of his own blood, with Mrs. Barclay insensible beside him. The coachman entered through the french window, as the room door was locked, and the key missing. A third person must have entered the room by the french window also, for five footmarks were discovered outside, and traces of another intruder, a small animal. "Neither dog, nor cat, nor monkey, nor any creature that we are familiar with," says Holmes, measuring its prints.

What was this strange beast? Why had Mrs. Barclay been heard screaming at her husband: "You coward! Give me back my life."? The problem is to be solved by the wandering conjurer, Henry Wood, and well might Holmes tell him, "Your narrative is most interesting."

The Strand Magazine, 1893

THE RESIDENT PATIENT. Like Hall Pycroft, the stockbroker's clerk, Dr. Percy Trevelyan finds prosperity appearing suddenly before him when least expected, in the form of a complete stranger with a proposition. Mr. Blessington's scheme is unconventional, yet logical enough; he will set up the impecunious but brilliant young doctor in West End practice, all expenses and pocket-money paid, in return for three-quarters of the takings. Other men invest in stocks and shares: why should he not put his money into a live investment? Also, his weak heart needs constant medical supervision, and it will be conveniently possible for him to make his own home in apartments above the consulting rooms.

It is not this, but subsequent occurrences, which lead Dr. Trevelyan to consult Sherlock Holmes. What is the significance of Mr. Blessington's alarm at reports of a West End burglary, and his hysteria upon discovering that his own room has been entered, even though nothing

of value has been touched? And what became of the Russian
nobleman who threw a cataleptic fit, and vanished?

The Strand Magazine, 1893

THE GREEK INTERPRETER.   So reticent has Holmes
always remained about the subject of his own family and
early life that it comes as no small shock to Watson to
hear him casually mention "my brother Mycroft". Yet
within an hour, Watson has been introduced to this
remarkable elder brother and has witnessed proof of
Holmes's magnanimous claim that, all things having been
equal, his brother might have surpassed even him as a
detective.

Watson is also introduced to Mycroft Holmes's fellow
clubman, Mr. Melas, a Greek interpreter with a strange
tale of having been abducted from his lodgings and per-
suaded to interpret a slate-pencil conversation with a
gagged and emaciated Athenian, who had managed to tell
him that he had been held prisoner for three weeks.
Another five minutes, and Melas might have wormed out
the whole story under the noses of their watching captors;
but a dramatic interruption by a tall, graceful woman had
cut short the interview in turmoil. Having found himself
liberated upon Clapham Common, Melas had wasted no
time in recounting his adventure to Mycroft Holmes, who
has since conducted as keen an investigation into it as his
natural indolence will permit. Mycroft is now thankful to
hand over the case to his more energetic younger brother.
Melas again disappears, but Holmes and Watson have
sufficient information to enable them to forestall one
murder, if not another.

The Strand Magazine, 1893

THE NAVAL TREATY.   Watson's school-friend, Percy
Phelps, enjoyed a flying start in the Civil Service, thanks
to an accident of birth. He has now come to regret ever

having *been* born, let alone having prospered in the Foreign Office. Entrusted by the Foreign Minister, his own uncle, with the copying of the vital naval treaty between England and Italy, Phelps had remained alone in his office one evening to get on with the work. Having stepped out for a moment to waken a dozing commissionaire to make him coffee, he had been horrified to hear the bell ringing from the room he had only just left unoccupied. Hurrying back he had found the room still empty, but the treaty gone. The windows, thirty feet from the ground, were fastened on the inside; there were no footmarks on the cream linoleum, although it had been raining outside for several hours. And what manner of thief would ring the bell to announce his presence and limit still further the time in which to make his escape? Little wonder that poor Phelps's mind had given temporarily under the strain. Even now, in convalescence, he must endure two further shocks—one in his own sick-room, and the other at the breakfast table of 221B, Baker Street.

The Strand Magazine, 1893

'Phelps raised the cover'

The Naval Treaty

'The death of Sherlock Holmes'

The Final Problem

THE FINAL PROBLEM. Only in retort to the recently published letter of Colonel James Moriarty in defence of his brother's memory can the despondent Watson bear to set down the particulars of the most devastating day he has ever lived.

He recalls how struck he had been one April evening by the increased thinness and pallor of Holmes, and by his friend's uncharacteristic suggestion that they should leave at once on a seemingly aimless Continental holiday. Only when Holmes had told him of the drawn-out battle of wits in which he had been engaged, and spoken the name of Professor Moriarty to him for the first time, had he come near to understanding the all-or-nothing nature of the problem the physical and mental demands of which taxed to the utmost even those almost superhuman resources.

Getting clear of the country, with Moriarty in close attendance, had proved a hectic endeavour; but, recalls Watson wistfully, there had followed a charming week in the Valley of the Rhone, shadowed though it had been by the news of a fire at 221B, Baker Street, and, even worse, the escape of Moriarty through the police net which Holmes's efforts had enabled to be drawn successfully about the rest of his organization. Then—on May 4th, 1891, most fateful of days—there had been that detour to view the falls of Reichenbach, where a messenger had come running and Watson, all unwittingly, had retraced his steps to assist a fellow countrywoman *in extremis*, turning briefly on his way to glimpse his friend for "the last that I was ever destined to see of him in this world".

The Strand Magazine, 1893

THE HOUND OF THE BASKERVILLES. "Mr. Holmes, they were the footprints of a gigantic hound!"

Dr. James Mortimer sinks his voice almost to a whisper as he tells Holmes and Watson of the sudden and mysterious death of Sir Charles Baskerville, of Baskerville

'Holmes emptied five barrels of his revolver into the creature's flank'
The Hound of the Baskervilles

Hall, Dartmoor, Devon. He has been found dead with no signs of violence, but 'an incredible facial distortion', which local rumour ascribed to death from shock; for the Baskervilles lie under the curse of the Hound, a terrible ghostly beast which slew the wicked Hugo Baskerville about 1648 and has since literally dogged his descendants' footsteps and hounded them to their doom. "I have hitherto confined my investigations to this world," Holmes muses; but he tells Dr. Mortimer to bring the young heir, Sir Henry Baskerville, to 221B, Baker Street. Sir Henry proves to be a realistic and sturdy young man who has spent most of his life in Canada and the States. Such small matters as a boot missing from his hotel room, and a letter warning him to 'keep away from the moor', are insufficient to deter him from taking up his inheritance.

Holmes is too occupied to go down to Devon and sends Watson with Sir Henry. Watson is daunted by the grim atmosphere of the Moor and the somewhat cheerless Hall, but is given a cordial welcome by Mr. and Mrs. Barrymore, its butler and housekeeper. Yet Barrymore is on Holmes's list of suspects, as he has inherited some money under the late Sir Charles's will; and the woman Watson hears weeping in the night can only be Mrs. Barrymore. Next day Watson meets a neighbour, Mr. Stapleton, a naturalist, and his beautiful sister, who warns Watson to go back to London. On the edge of the great Grimpen Mire, he hears a long, low moan, which Stapleton says is the Hound of the Baskervilles calling for its prey. The Hound is evidently not alone on the Moor. A convict is in hiding there. But it is not until Watson has run to earth a further figure he has glimpsed upon the Moor that he can penetrate to the heart of the mystery.

The Strand Magazine, August, 1901–April, 1902

'I crept forward and looked across at the familiar window'
The Empty House

THE EMPTY HOUSE. Three years after the death of Sherlock Holmes, Watson still retains the interest in criminal matters so deeply imbued in him by his much-lamented friend. Like all London, he finds the circumstances of the murder of the Hon. Ronald Adair as inexplicable as they are fascinating. The young man has been shot in his locked room in the house which he shared with his mother and sister in Park Lane. While mingling with the loungers opposite the house, listening to their theories and trying in vain to construct one of his own, Watson incurs the opprobrium of an elderly, deformed man for accidentally knocking several books out of his hands. Having retraced his steps home he has scarcely been five minutes in his study when the strange old bookman is shown in to begin a line of hard sales talk.

Looking away momentarily to glance at one of his book-shelves, Watson turns back again to find the old man transformed into a smiling Sherlock Holmes. For the first time in his life, Watson faints. Restored, he finds that it is indeed Holmes who has loosened his tie and administered brandy. He hears a well-nigh incredible account of escape from the brink of death and of subsequent wanderings in many lands, and is delighted to be invited once more to share in an investigation which this time will take the two adventurers to an empty house immediately opposite their former Baker Street quarters. Here Watson will meet another old Indian hand, Colonel Sebastian Moran, "the best heavy game shot that our Eastern Empire has ever produced", and—since the death of Moriarty—the most dangerous man in London.

The Strand Magazine, 1903

THE NORWOOD BUILDER. The police are already hard upon the heels of the frantic young solicitor, John Hector McFarlane, when he bursts unannounced into the parlour of 221B, Baker Street. He has barely begun to tell a tale which will stifle for a while Holmes's recurrent plaint that crime is not what it was since the death of Moriarty, before Inspector Lestrade arrives to arrest him for the murder of Jonas Oldacre, a retired builder, of Lower Norwood, whose charred remains have been discovered in a burnt-out timber stack. With reservations,

'*A wild-eyed and frantic young man burst into the room*'
The Norwood Builder

Holmes is for once inclined to concede that Lestrade has a convincing case. McFarlane was undeniably Oldacre's last visitor before his death. His bloodstained stick has been found at the scene of the crime; and the matter seems to be clinched by the accused's admission that he had just drawn up a will for Oldacre in which the retired builder had left him most of what he owned. But even a Scotland Yard investigator can have too much of a good thing—in this instance the murderer's bloodstained thumb-print which somehow contrived to be made *after* his arrest. Holmes deduces a missing witness and resorts to arson to flush him from cover.

The Strand Magazine, 1903

THE DANCING MEN. "Every problem becomes very childish when once it is explained to you," Holmes declares, passing Watson a sheet of paper bearing a drawing of tiny figures of dancing men, crudely sketched, in various positions of signalling. Mr. Hilton Cubitt, of Norfolk, has received 'this little conundrum'. A similar series of drawings has been frightening his American wife Elsie nearly to death recently, though she will not tell him why. Nor has she told her trusting husband anything of her past or of her people, for there have been some disagreeable associations which she wishes to forget. But now she has become "like a woman in a dream, half dazed, and with terror always lurking in her eyes", and Hilton Cubitt has decided to ask Holmes to track down whatever is frightening her.

After two hours' study of the dancing men, Holmes springs up with a cry of satisfaction, writes a long telegram, and observes."If my answer to this is as I hope, you will have a very pretty case to add to your collection, Watson". But the case proves to be anything but pretty: tragedy moves too swiftly, even for Sherlock Holmes.

The Strand Magazine, 1903

THE SOLITARY CYCLIST. On Saturday, April 23rd, 1895, Miss Violet Smith interrupts Holmes in the middle of a very abstruse and complicated problem. Miss Smith's problem may be more trivial, but it is intriguing.

8—S.H.C.

'Holmes clapped a pistol to his head and Martin slipped
the handcuffs over his wrists'

The Dancing Men

Some time ago, she and her widowed mother had been surprised to see an advertisement in *The Times* inquiring for their whereabouts. This, they found, had been inserted by a Mr. Carruthers and a Mr. Woodley, home from South Africa, where they had met Miss Smith's Uncle Ralph, of whom the Smiths had heard nothing since he went there twenty-five years before. He had died poor in Johannesburg, said Carruthers and Woodley, but had asked them with his last breath to find Miss Smith and her mother and see that they were in no want. Carruthers, true to his trust, had offered Miss Smith a well-paid post teaching music to his young daughter at his home, Chiltern Grange, near Farnham in Surrey. This had proved a very pleasant occupation until Mr. Woodley came for a week's visit.

Recently, every Saturday, when bicycling along a lonely road to catch a train to her mother's, in London, Miss Smith has kept catching sight of another cyclist following her—a man with a short dark beard. He always appears at the same point, and disappears without trace. Some deep intrigue clearly surrounds Miss Smith.

Holmes employs his skill as a boxer in dealing with the unsavoury Woodley, and a dramatic race against time ends in the cry: "You're too late. She's my wife!" and the rejoinder: "No, she's your widow", followed by the crack of a revolver.

The Strand Magazine, 1904

THE PRIORY SCHOOL. Holmes and Watson have witnessed many dramatic entries to their rooms at No. 221B but none more so than that of Dr. Thorneycroft Huxtable, a North of England headmaster, whose first action is to fall to the floor insensible. Restored with Watson's never-failing physic, brandy, he begs their assistance in averting scandal and ruin following the disappearance from his school of the young Lord Saltire. The school's

'*A straight left against a slogging ruffian*'

The Solitary Cyclist

German master has also disappeared and the police have drawn the obvious conclusion that the case is one of abduction.

Having heard that the German's departure had been by bicycle, Holmes is inclined to look further than this: as far, in fact, as the neighbourhood of the Priory School itself, a wilderness of rolling moorland with a few sheep as virtually its only inhabitants. A day's tracking is

'*The heavy white face was seamed with lines of trouble*'

The Priory School

evidently too much for Holmes, who goes lame and has to be helped by Watson to a remote inn, in search of transport.

Holmes muses upon the cow-tracks he has seen on a moor where no cows are, observes the Duke of Holdernesse's secretary in unlikely surroundings, and finds grounds for berating the nobleman in his own ducal hall.

The Strand Magazine, 1904

BLACK PETER.   In the back room of a butcher's shop a
dead pig swings from a hook in the ceiling, and a gentleman in his shirt-sleeves stabs furiously at it with a huge
spear. Sherlock Holmes is making a practical experiment
which may explain the death of Captain Peter Carey—
"flushed with drink and as savage as a dangerous beast"
on Tuesday, transfixed to the wall of his 'cabin' with a
heavy harpoon by Wednesday morning. Perhaps it is as
well that in this year of '95, Holmes (Watson tells us) is
at the peak of his physical as well as his mental powers.
Running through a pig at a single blow, he discovers, is
beyond even his super-normal capabilities, one of the few
significant facts in a case where the only apparent clues are
a bottle of rum and two empty glasses, a sealskin tobacco
pouch bearing the initials 'P.C.', and a notebook containing
what seem to be Stock Exchange figures.

In spite of his annoyance that so much time has been
squandered in incomplete inquiries by the police, Holmes
is clearly preoccupied by the case. Watson knows better
than to ask for details before they have been volunteered;
but the fact that several rough-looking men have been
calling at 221B to ask for a Captain Basil is a sure sign that
something is on hand. One of them, a harpooner of gigantic
physique, seems likely to provide the answer to the pig-
sticking problem, and Holmes advises Watson to put his
revolver within easy reach.

The Strand Magazine, 1904

CHARLES AUGUSTUS MILVERTON.   Having heard
Holmes term Charles Augustus Milverton the worst man
in London, Watson is surprised to learn that so viperous
a person is about to call on them by invitation. When the
interview takes place he can only stand by and seethe
helplessly as Holmes is forced to accept mortification and
defeat. For Holmes knows the weakness of his—or rather,
his client's—position. Milverton has lately come into

'You couldn't come at any other time—eh?'

Charles Augustus Milverton

possession of certain letters written indiscreetly to a young man by Lady Eva Brackwell, the most beautiful debutante of the previous season, who is to be married to the Earl of Dovercourt in a fortnight's time. Exposure will mean social ruin and an end to the match. Milverton's demands in exchange for the letters are exorbitant and Holmes is helpless to bargain with him.

Desperate measures are needed, and those adopted by Holmes are desperate indeed. Casting aside a lifetime's distaste for women, he becomes engaged to a housemaid named Agatha, enters the plumbing trade, and, for once, declines to lend the police his assistance in a murder investigation.

The Strand Magazine, 1904

THE SIX NAPOLEONS.   Why should Morse Hudson's shop in the Kennington Road be visited by a man who smashes a plaster bust of Napoleon upon the counter, and runs away? Why should a burglary at the house of Dr. Barnicot of Brixton, the collector of Napoleonic relics, be carried out solely for the purpose of removing and smashing another plaster cast of the Emperor's head, one of two duplicates bought from Morse Hudson? And why should the second duplicate, kept at his surgery, be smashed to atoms? These questions, which so puzzle Inspector Lestrade, seem to Holmes worth following up. Somewhere there is an interesting monomaniac; perhaps a man whose ancestors have suffered during the Napoleonic Wars. However, he leaves it to Lestrade to investigate, until Mr. Horace Harker, a journalist, reports that *his* bust of Napoleon has been stolen, and that in pursuit of the thief he has stumbled over the dead body of a man, with a great gash in its throat.

"Now, Watson," says Holmes, "I think that we shall find we have a long and rather complex day's work before us." They have. It is the indignant and voluble Morse

'*With the bound of a tiger Holmes was on his back*'

The Six Napoleons

Hudson who gives them a clue to the identity of the dead man and possibly to that of the iconoclast.

The Strand Magazine, 1904

THE THREE STUDENTS.   For all his complaints about the decline in criminal enterprise and the lack of worthwhile cases demanding his attention, Sherlock Holmes is just occasionally displeased to be disturbed from his other pursuits. He is downright surly, for instance, when, in the midst of laborious researches into Early English charters in 'one of our great University towns', he is interrupted by the tutor and lecturer at the College of St. Luke's, Mr. Hilton Soames, with some trifling matter of a Greek examination paper. Yet it is not long before his interest is aroused and his spirits restored. An important examination, with valuable rewards, is impending. The question papers, left confidently lying behind locked doors, have been disturbed: the simple question is, by which of three candidates most likely to have gained access to them—the poor but athletic son of a ruined father; the brilliant but dissipated idler; or the inscrutable Indian, weak in Greek? The only material clues appear to be some pencil shavings and some black, doughy pellets, roughly pyramidal in shape and flecked with grains of sawdust. By turning himself out of bed at the untimely hour of six and covering at least five miles in the course of two hours' hard work Holmes soon frees himself to return to his own laborious studies.

The Strand Magazine, 1904

THE GOLDEN PINCE-NEZ.   A November wind howls down Baker Street and the rain beats fiercely against the windows of No. 221B as a solitary cab splashes its way from the Oxford Street end. Young Stanley Hopkins, of the Yard, is about to disturb two gentlemen's quiet with his tale of the death of young Willoughby Smith, at Yoxley Old Place, in Kent.

Willoughby Smith had been secretary to Professor Coram, an elderly invalid whose quiet bachelor household contains no suspicious elements. Yet the secretary has been found in the professor's study, dying of a deep wound in the carotid artery, inflicted with a small sealing-wax knife. To the maid who found him he could murmur only one enigmatic sentence: "The professor . . . it was she." Not much to go upon: but it requires only Hopkins's account of the crime and its setting to enable Holmes to scribble upon a piece of paper a description of a person whom he has never seen, but for whom they would do well to seek.

The Strand Magazine, 1904

THE MISSING THREE-QUARTER. The Cambridge Rugby team faces downfall: its right-wing three-quarter, Godfrey Staunton, has disappeared, the night before the 'Varsity meets Oxford in the field. The Cambridge skipper, Cyril Overton, has been sent along by Scotland Yard to consult Holmes, a man ignorant of Rugby football and its giants. At Bentley's Private Hotel in London the previous night Staunton had been pale and 'bothered', his captain recalls. Perhaps this had something to do with a note delivered to him by a rough-looking man, with whom he had gone off towards the Strand, since when no word has been received from him. As Holmes is deciphering on a piece of hotel blotting-paper the words '. . . stand by us for God's sake', part of a telegram sent by Staunton, a shabby little old man appears in the doorway. It is Lord Mount-James, the rich old relative of the missing man. He knows nothing of his nephew's whereabouts either; so with only the truncated telegram for a clue, Holmes sets out for the telegraph-office and a piece of information which takes him and Watson to the starting-point for a journey—King's Cross Station.

The Strand Magazine, 1904

THE ABBEY GRANGE. According to Watson the adventure of the Abbey Grange was to have been the last adventure of Sherlock Holmes he intended to communicate to the public. Holmes, we learn, has been showing increased resistance to the publication of his experiences: and, for once, we are perhaps not so surprised. "What were these commonplace rogues that he should soil his hands with them? An abstruse and learned specialist who finds that he has been called in for a case of measles would experience something of the annoyance which I read in my friend's eyes."

Lady Brackenstall had disturbed the three members of the Randall gang breaking into her house. They had bound her, insensible, to a chair, with a bell-rope, and when Sir Eustace himself had appeared upon the scene had beaten out his brains with a blow vicious enough to bend a stout poker, departing with some pieces of silver after pausing only to refresh themselves from a bottle of excellent vintage. Only too painfully does Holmes now recollect shrugging his shoulders upon the case and taking the first train back to London. How could he have overlooked the significance of the half-empty bottle, the three wine glasses, and the fact that the lady was tied to the chair at all? But the telling clue lay all the time in Lady Brackenstall's Australian origins and associations.

The Strand Magazine, 1904

THE SECOND STAIN. Even Sherlock Holmes can have had few more illustrious visitors than Lord Bellinger, twice Premier of Britain, and the Right Honourable Trelawney Hope, Secretary for European Affairs. Together they are come to beg him to recover a missing document whose publication might lead to European complications of the utmost moment. Trelawney Hope had received the letter from a foreign potentate six days before, and locked it in a dispatch-box in his bedroom, without disclosing its presence to anyone in the house. Both he and his wife are convinced that no one could have entered the room during the night; yet the paper is gone, and the position is grave. Holmes takes a sombre view.

"You think, sir, that unless this document is recovered there will be war?"

"I think it is very probable."

"Then, sir, prepare for war."

When his visitors have left it occurs to Holmes that of three men who might have been bold enough to steal the paper, perhaps the likeliest is Eduardo Lucas, of Godolphin Street, Westminster. But Watson, that earnest student of the daily press, informs him that Lucas has just been murdered. So begins 'the most important international case that Holmes had ever been called upon to handle.'

The Strand Magazine, 1904

THE VALLEY OF FEAR.   Holmes has received a letter in cypher, of which the only readable words are 'DOUGLAS' and 'BIRLSTONE'. It is from one of his informants, named Porlock, an agent of Professor Moriarty—"the greatest schemer of all time . . . the controlling brain of the underworld". Holmes finds the clue to the cypher in *Whitaker's Almanack*, and translates the message as an urgent summons to Birlstone, Sussex, where one Douglas is in danger. At that moment Inspector MacDonald of Scotland Yard arrives, with the startling news that Mr. Douglas, of Birlstone Manor House, has been horribly murdered that morning. Holmes is not altogether surprised, and senses an interesting case: "I can only see two things for certain at present: a great brain in London and a dead man in Sussex. It's the chain between that we are going to trace."

At Birlstone, Holmes and Watson learn that the late

John Douglas had been an American, amiable and popular,
indifferent to danger. His wife is English. At the time of
the murder they were entertaining a friend, Mr. Cecil
James Barker, and he it was who discovered the body of
his host with the head almost blown to pieces by a sawn-off
shotgun. Beside it lay a card with 'V.V. 341' scrawled on
it in ink, and the wedding-ring had been removed from
the corpse's hand. Holmes notes a branded sign on
Douglas's forearm, and the fact that of a pair of dumb-bells
with which Douglas used to exercise only one is now to
be found. He is also struck by the curious attitude of
Barker, and the fact that Mrs. Douglas does not give the
impression of being an inconsolable widow. Darkness and
Dr. Watson's umbrella provide keys to the problem and
help to disclose a tale of black doings in the American
coalfields.

The Strand Magazine,
September 1914–April 1915

WISTERIA LODGE. Mr. John Scott Eccles is a
bachelor of a sociable turn. This had led to his receiving
and accepting an invitation to Wisteria Lodge, between
Esher and Oxshott, in Surrey, the house of Garcia, a young
Spaniard. It had turned out to be a depressing house, and
Mr. Eccles's first evening there was not enlivened by his
host's receiving a note which caused him to retreat into
distraction and gloom. Next morning, the guest awoke,
rang for Garcia's Spanish servant, received no response,
and hurried downstairs—to find himself alone in the house.
Such was his visit to Wisteria Lodge, which led him to
consult Sherlock Holmes, and which also leads the police
to consult Mr. Eccles—for Garcia has been found murdered on Oxshott Common, his head smashed to pulp, and
a letter from Eccles in his pocket.

Holmes and Watson visit the Bull at Esher, hear a
constable's tale of a terrible face at a window, discover

some gruesome objects, and so find themselves upon the trail of the Tiger of San Pedro, of hateful memory. "A chaotic case, my dear Watson."

Collier's (U.S.A.), August, 1908
The Strand Magazine, September-October, 1908

THE CARDBOARD BOX. Of all potential recipients of postal packets containing two freshly severed human ears, one of the least likely would have been considered Miss Susan Cushing, a middle-aged maiden lady living quietly in Croydon. But Miss Cushing once had medical students lodging with her, and worse than ears have been smuggled out of dissecting rooms.

The Cardboard Box

Holmes, however, is pleased to accept Inspector Lestrade's invitation to look into the case; and having seen and sniffed at the string with which the grisly parcel had been secured, and closely observed the wrapping paper and the address printed thereon ("Done with a broad-pointed pen, probably a J, and with very inferior ink"), he is only too ready to have a word with the outraged Miss Cushing herself. One glance at her profile is virtually enough. Holmes feels free to relax with a bottle of claret and entertain Watson with anecdotes of Paganini while awaiting the answer to a telegram; having received it he can assure Lestrade that no practical joke, but a shocking crime, has been committed, and, for extra good measure, tells him the murderer's name.

The Strand Magazine, 1893

THE RED CIRCLE. Mrs. Warren's lodger was giving her trouble. He paid well, certainly—five pounds a week was handsome for rooms in Great Orme Street, near the British Museum—but his habits were most undesirable. He had offered a high rent on condition that he should be absolutely undisturbed, even his meals being left outside his sitting-room. Any extra instructions for Mrs. Warren would be in the form of printed pencil messages. Reasonable enough, Holmes tells her when she consults him. But when Mrs. Warren's husband is bundled into a cab, driven for an hour, and tipped out on to Hampstead Heath by two unseen assailants, Holmes's obvious conclusion is that the two men mistook the unfortunate Mr. Warren for the lodger. It is time, he thinks, that a little more was known about someone interesting enough to be abducted; and accordingly he and Watson station themselves behind Mrs. Warren's boxroom door with a mirror that will show them the lodger when he appears to collect his tray; but it is not the bearded, moustached face they had expected.

A code of signals is solved, and a representative of Pinkerton's American Detective Agency appears on the scene, before Mrs. Warren's troubles are cleared up.

The Strand Magazine, 1911

THE BRUCE-PARTINGTON PLANS. A young man taking his fiancée to a London theatre one murky evening in 1895 suddenly relinquishes her arm and, without a word of explanation, vanishes into the fog. He does not return. She has, in fact, just seen him for the last time. The following morning his body is found beside the track of the Underground railway, just outside Aldgate station. The head is badly crushed, seemingly from a fall from a train.

It is the contents of the dead man's pockets which lead Mycroft Holmes, in his official capacity, to summon his brother Sherlock into urgent investigation. They include the plans of the Bruce-Partington submarine, the most jealously guarded of all government secrets. The plans have been under elaborate guard at Woolwich Arsenal, where the deceased worked as a junior clerk.

How they came to be in his possession—and, more pressing still, where the three most important of the ten documents have disappeared to—it is Holmes's task to discover. The heads of his nation await his solution, and at Windsor an old lady sends out for an emerald tie-pin.

The Strand Magazine, 1908

THE DYING DETECTIVE. Mrs. Hudson, far from her Baker Street domain, is a surprise caller at Watson's rooms. She carries alarming news: Sherlock Holmes lies at the point of death. Since returning from working on a case amongst Chinese sailors in a riverside alley at Rotherhithe, he has taken neither food nor drink, but has only lain in bed, babbling like a child and declining visibly, yet refusing medical aid.

The appearance of the faithful Watson at his bedside does nothing to comfort him. The doctor, willing for the sake of his friend to risk contact with a disease as deadly and obscure as Tapanuli fever or the black Formosa corruption, hears himself rebuffed as a mere general practitioner, of mediocre qualifications. He does at least earn a little praise for his qualities as a messenger, summoning to the deathbed Mr. Culverton Smith, formerly of Sumatra, the one man with the knowledge—though not necessarily the inclination—to effect a cure.

Colliers (U.S.A.), November, 1913
The Strand Magazine, December, 1913

THE DISAPPEARANCE OF LADY FRANCES CARFAX. To Watson, who for a few days past has been feeling rheumaticky and old, the suggestion of a trip to Lausanne, with all expenses paid, is a glowing alternative to the mere Turkish bath. Reluctant to provoke unhealthy excitement among the criminal classes by leaving London himself, Holmes sends him off on the lone trail of the Lady Frances Carfax, last heard of travelling unaccompanied on the Continent with the remains of the valuable family jewellery amongst her baggage. Watson, unfortunately, has assimilated little of the art of detection in his association with Holmes, and after narrowly escaping a thrashing at the hands of his chief suspect, and failing to answer a vital, though (to him) seemingly flippant inquiry about a missionary's left ear, he is bidden back to London before he can blunder further.

Before the case is over, though, poor Watson has the satisfaction of hearing Holmes ask: "What has become of any brains that God has given me?" It really seems that 'Holy' Peters has been too cunning for him; and before Holmes has recognized the significance of a coffin built for two, time has almost run out.

The Strand Magazine, 1911

THE DEVIL'S FOOT. 'Why not tell them of the Cornish horror—strangest case I have handled'—telegraphed Holmes to Watson. He did not exaggerate.

It is spring, 1897. Holmes has been overworking, and is taking a rest-cure in a small cottage near Poldhu Bay, on the coast of Cornwall. It is not to be a very restful rest-cure, from the moment that two visitors arrive—the vicar of the near-by hamlet of Tredannick Wollas, and Mr. Mortimer Tregennis, who occupies rooms in the vicarage. Holmes and Watson hear a terrible story. The previous evening, Mr. Tregennis had been playing cards with his two brothers and his sister Brenda, at their house of Tredannick Wartha. All had been well when he left them; but the next morning they had been discovered still seated round the card-table, Brenda stone-dead and her two brothers laughing, shouting and singing in utter dementia.

Beyond the fact that a fire had been lit on a spring evening, Holmes notes nothing remarkable at the scene of the crime. He ponders on the problem as he and Watson walk on the cliffs and search for flint arrows. When they return to the cottage, another visitor awaits them—none other than Dr. Leon Sterndale, the great lion-hunter and explorer. More sinister and tragic events are impending, and Holmes and Watson themselves are to run into terrible danger.

The Strand Magazine, 1910

His Last Bow. It is August, 1914. Von Bork, that powerful and elusive German agent who has been giving His Majesty's Government so much trouble, is soon to leave his cliff-top dwelling—'the centre of half the mischief in England'—and return to Berlin. Only one item is wanting to complete his haul—a document concerning naval signals. "Thanks to my cheque-book and the good Altamont all will be well tonight," Von Bork anticipates. And here comes this Altamont—the bitter, touchy, England-hating Irish American who covers his espionage activities by posing as a motor expert. He springs from his car waving a small brown-paper parcel above his head: "You can give me the glad hand tonight, Mister, I'm bringing home the bacon at last." Behind him, his chauffeur, a heavily built, elderly man, with a grey moustache, settles down to wait. It seems that Britain's enemies are triumphant. But Sherlock Holmes has a last bow to take.

The Strand Magazine, 1917

THE ILLUSTRIOUS CLIENT.   An unnamed client is not to Holmes's taste, but there are enough interesting features in the case brought to him by Sir James Damery to overcome any disinclination. The infatuation which the notorious Baron Adelbert Gruner has managed to inspire in the breast of the daughter of so fine an old soldier as General de Merville is, to Holmes's mind as much as to Damery's, something which must be cut short as swiftly and ruthlessly as possible.

Holmes's liking for meeting an adversary eye to eye, in order to read his quality for himself, takes him to a fruitless meeting with the baron. His attempt to deal directly with the endangered young lady is not only unsuccessful, but disastrous. The baron's threat to meet interference with his own means had been no empty one, and Watson stands stunned near Charing Cross Station to read a newspaper placard: 'MURDEROUS ATTACK UPON SHERLOCK HOLMES'. Within hours the nation learns that the great detective is unlikely to last out the week, as Watson obeys a deathbed order to make a twenty-four hours' study of Chinese ceramics, and Miss Kitty Winter anticipates a long-awaited revenge.

Collier's (U.S.A.), November, 1924
The Strand Magazine, February-March, 1925

THE BLANCHED SOLDIER.   Yielding at last to Watson's persuasion, Holmes recounts one of his own cases, beginning with a recollection of a visit from a bronzed, upstanding young ex-soldier, James M. Dodd, come to solicit his aid in finding a former comrade-in-arms, Godfrey Emsworth. Since they became separated in South Africa they have had little communication, and Dodd's recent inquiries of his friend's parents have met with blunt evasion. For all this, he can swear that he has had one momentary glimpse of Godfrey, a furtive figure at a window at night, more deadly pale than mortal man was ever before.

Elementary as this problem is to Holmes, he goes willingly enough to the scene of this ghastly visitation— Godfrey Emsworth's home. Before the master of the house can have him removed from the premises he has scribbled a single word on a sheet of paper—a word which removes immediately from old Colonel Emsworth's face all expression save amazement.

Liberty Magazine (U.S.A.), October, 1926
The Strand Magazine, November, 1926

THE MAZARIN STONE. Dropping into his erstwhile home, Watson is not surprised to learn from Billy, the page-boy, that Holmes is in bed asleep—at seven in the evening of a lovely summer's day. Billy tells him that his master has been hard at it. The Prime Minister and Home Secretary, no less, have recently been 'sitting on that very sofa', for the recovery of the missing Crown Diamond is a matter of national urgency. An effigy of Holmes, seated, apparently reading, in the window, recalls to Watson the case of *The Empty House* and Holmes appears to confirm cheerfully that he is in imminent expectation of an attempt upon his life, in which, again, an air-gun figures. When Billy returns to announce that the would-be assassin is at the door, Watson is as willing as of old to clear for action. Instead, urged by Holmes, he reluctantly leaves to find a cab to Scotland Yard, convinced that he is abandoning his old comrade to an untimely fate at the hands of Count Negretto Sylvius. Holmes, however, sees him off undismayed. That great music-lover feels confident in the ability of the Hoffmann *Barcarolle* to soothe even so savage a breast as this.

The Strand Magazine, 1921

THE THREE GABLES. "Which of you genelmen is Masser Holmes?" is the greeting, as he enters the sitting-room of 221B, Baker Street, of a huge, dark-skinned figure in a loud grey check suit and flowing salmon-coloured tie. If Steve Dixie does not recognize Sherlock Holmes, Holmes recognizes him and reminds the negro boxer that he is aware of his connections with Barney Stockdale and the Spencer John gang. Dixie's warning, "I've a friend that's interested out Harrow way, and he don't intend to have no buttin' in by you," seems to link up with an appeal for help which Holmes has received from Mrs. Mary Maberley, of Harrow Weald.

Mrs. Maberley is the widowed mother of Douglas Maberley, a brilliant young diplomat who had been Attaché at Rome before his death from pneumonia—the outcome, according to his mother, of a love affair with "a woman—or a fiend". But this is not her present cause for concern. A house agent, acting on behalf of an unnamed client, has offered a good price for her house and furniture complete; but her solicitor has warned her that by accepting it she will lose the right to remove any object, however personal, from the house. While Mrs. Maberley is telling him this, Holmes's sharp ear catches the sound of wheezy breathing outside the door and in a matter of moments he has established a further link with the unscrupulous Barney Stockdale.

Liberty Magazine (U.S.A.), September, 1926
The Strand Magazine, October, 1926

THE SUSSEX VAMPIRE. "What do we know about vampires?" asks Holmes of Watson, having received a curious communication from a firm of solicitors whose client, Mr. Robert Ferguson, has approached them on the subject. A short study of his notes on vampirism persuades Holmes that Mr. Ferguson cannot be taken very seriously, whatever his trouble. But a letter from Ferguson, who proves to be an old friend of Watson's, alters his decision.

Ferguson has been twice married, and has a son of fifteen by his first wife and another of eleven months by his second wife, a Peruvian lady. Though normally of gentle disposition, and devoted to her husband, Mrs. Ferguson has lately been causing him anxiety by her violent conduct towards Jacky, the elder boy, and by what appear to be murderous attacks on her own baby son. The nurse has found her apparently biting the child's neck, from which a stream of blood was running. Ferguson has accused her, and she has taken refuge in her room.

Holmes and Watson travel to Lamberley, in Sussex, and meet the Ferguson family: the beautiful distracted wife, who begs for her baby, but will give no explanation of her conduct; Jacky, the crippled boy; and the baby whose neck is still marked by an angry scar. There is a dog, too, whose condition seems to interest Holmes.

"It must be an exceedingly delicate and complex affair from your point of view," says Ferguson; but Holmes smiles. Delicate, yes, but complex, not at all.

Hearst's International Magazine (U.S.A.), January, 1924
The Strand Magazine, January, 1924

THE THREE GARRIDEBS. "If you can lay your hand upon a Garrideb, there's money in it," Holmes has told Watson. An American millionaire of that name, it seems, has left the whole of his estate, valued at some $15,000,000 to be shared equally between any three males named Garrideb; and one of the few, John Garrideb, a fellow American, is hotly in search of two others. He has already discovered one, Nathan Garrideb, who, like himself, has unfortunately no male relative eligible to complete the trio and make them all rich. Nathan's bright idea has been to engage the services of Sherlock Holmes to complete the search. It seems, however, that his assistance will not be necessary after all: John Garrideb has found in a newspaper the advertisement of one Howard Garrideb, constructor of agricultural machinery in Birmingham.

Collier's Magazine (U.S.A.), October, 1924
The Strand Magazine, January, 1925

THOR BRIDGE.   After months of professional stagnation, Holmes is cheerful once more. He has a client, Mr. J. Neil Gibson, the millionaire gold king from America, now the owner of Thor Place, a considerable estate in Hampshire. This formidable tycoon is seeking aid, not for himself, but for the governess of his two young children, Miss Grace Dunbar. Gibson's faded tropical plant of a wife has been discovered late at night in the grounds of Thor Place, clad in a dinner dress, with a shawl over her shoulders and a revolver bullet through her brain. A revolver with one discharged chamber has been found in the wardrobe of Miss Dunbar, who, from her employer's attitude towards her, has seemed for some time to be the likeliest successor to his wife in the event of her death.

The evidence against her is strong, and Holmes's distaste for her employer is marked: also, disuse has perhaps rendered his mind sluggish. But an interview with the accused woman and a few blows of his cane upon the parapet of a bridge are enough to set him proclaiming that the case is going to make England ring, and he reminds Watson to bring along his revolver.

The Strand Magazine, 1922

THE CREEPING MAN.   A curious change seems to have come over Professor Presbury since his engagement, at the age of sixty-one, to the young daughter of one of his colleagues. His lectures remain as brilliant as ever, but there is a new air of the furtive and sly about him. He no longer confides in his secretary, Trevor Bennett, whom he had always treated like a son or younger brother; and on two recent occasions his faithful wolf-hound, Roy, has made a point of trying to bite his master.

The change seems to date from an unexplained trip away from home, about which all that is known is that he spent some time in Prague. A Continental tour is suggested by a carved box of a characteristic German type which he brought back with him, and which now lies securely locked and not to be touched in his instrument cupboard. But there are even further strange features for Sherlock Holmes to grapple with in one of the last cases of his career: such as secret letters, written in an illiterate hand, from an address in East London; and the somewhat excessive nature of the professor's wooing.

The Strand Magazine, 1923

THE LION'S MANE. Taking the air along the Channel cliffs one morning in his retirement, Holmes finds himself precipitated into as baffling a mystery as any from his working years. Fitzroy Macpherson, the science master of a local school, staggers up from the beach, where he has been for a swim, collapses, and dies, crying out, "The lion's mane!" He is only half dressed, and his back is covered with weals, as though he has been flogged mercilessly with some flexible wire scourge.

In so remote a part of Sussex there is no difficulty in singling out a suspect. The obvious choice is a fellow master, Ian Murdoch, whose ferocious temper had earlier led him to an act of violence against Macpherson's dog, and who, it transpires, had once been his rival in affection for the neighbourhood beauty, Maud Bellamy. That this same dog should die while the investigation is going on is less of a surprise to Holmes than a manifestation of 'the beautiful, faithful nature of dogs'. But why at precisely the same spot where his master met his death? A sacrifice to some revengeful feud . . .?

Liberty Magazine (U.S.A.), November, 1926
The Strand Magazine, December, 1926

THE VEILED LODGER. "The most terrible human tragedies were often involved in these cases which brought him the fewest personal opportunities," Watson remarks, citing the case of *The Veiled Lodger* as just such an instance.

Holmes is approached by a South Brixton landlady of his acquaintance to visit the lady lodger whose face she has glimpsed only once in seven years, but whose voice she has many times heard crying "Murder!" The mysterious lodger's name—Ronder—stirs Holmes's memory, and he is soon swishing through the leaves of the commonplace books in the corner to the account of the tragedy at Abbas Parva, in Berkshire, some years before, when the staff at Ronder's Wild Beast Show rushed from their tents to discover, by the light of their lanterns, their employer with the back of his head crushed in and his wife mutilated almost to the point of death by the North African lion which stood snarling over her. For once, however, Holmes is being summoned not to act, but to listen to a confession which succeeds in moving him to sympathy such as Watson has seldom known him to exhibit.

Liberty Magazine (U.S.A.), January, 1927
The Strand Magazine, February, 1927

SHOSCOMBE OLD PLACE. Shoscombe Prince is the best colt in England; and he needs to be if his owner, Sir Robert Norberton, is to escape ruin at the moneylenders' hands. Everything he possesses is wagered on the horse to win the Derby; to win, that is, if he is able even to run under Sir Robert's colours—and not a soul other than the impoverished gambler knows how reduced the likelihood of this has become.

No wonder, then, that Sir Robert has been behaving so strangely: the furtive trips to the old church crypt at night; the giving away of his sister's beloved spaniel. But Holmes's task is to discover the significance of rather more sinister manifestations: the human bone in the furnace, and the anachronistic contents of an eighteenth-century coffin.

It is his regard for the nobility of dogs that will lead him to the vital clue.

Liberty Magazine (U.S.A.), March, 1927
The Strand Magazine, April, 1927

THE RETIRED COLOURMAN.   "The old story, Watson, a treacherous friend and a fickle wife." These are what bring old Josiah Amberley, the retired colourman of Lewisham, to Holmes's consulting-room: for his young wife and her lover have vanished, and with them a large part of Mr. Amberley's life-savings. Watson understudies Holmes in the investigation of this case, visiting the neglected old house behind its high brick wall, where some clue to the vanished pair may lurk. He learns very little, but encounters a suspicious character—a man with a heavy moustache, tinted sun-glasses and a Masonic tie-pin.

A mysterious telegram from an Essex vicar takes Amberley and Watson on what seems to be a wild goose chase. The solution to the case of the retired colourman does not lie in rural Essex: it is in Lewisham, in the old house smelling of fresh paint. Holmes resorts to another of his skills: "Burglary has always been an alternative profession, had I cared to adopt it, and I have little doubt that I should have come to the front."

Liberty Magazine (U.S.A.), December, 1926
The Strand Magazine, January, 1927

A SAMPLER OF QUOTATIONS

'Come, Watson, come!' he cried. *'The game is afoot'*

The Abbey Grange

ON HOLMES

"He is a little queer in his ideas—an enthusiast in some branches of science. As far as I know he is a decent fellow enough. . . . I believe he is well up in anatomy, and he is a first-class chemist; but, as far as I know, he has never taken out any systematic medical classes. His studies are desultory and eccentric, but he has amassed a lot of out-of-the-way knowledge which would astonish his professors."—Stamford, *A Study in Scarlet*.

"Holmes is a little too scientific for my tastes—it approaches to cold-bloodedness. I could imagine his giving a friend a little pinch of the latest vegetable alkaloid, not out of malevolence, you understand, but simply out of a spirit of inquiry in order to have an accurate idea of the effects. To do him justice, I think that he would take it himself with the same readiness."—Stamford, *A Study in Scarlet*.

My surprise reached a climax . . . when I found accidentally that he was ignorant of the Copernican Theory and of the composition of the Solar System. "You appear to be astonished," he said. . . . "Now that I do know it I shall do my best to forget it . . . depend upon it there comes a time when for every addition of knowledge you forget something that you knew before. It is of the highest importance, therefore, not to have useless facts elbowing out the useful ones."

"But the Solar System!" I protested.

"What the deuce is it to me? . . . You say that we go round the sun. If we went round the moon it would not make a pennyworth of difference to me or to my work."—*A Study in Scarlet*.

I enumerated in my own mind all the various points upon which he had shown me that he was exceptionally well informed. I even took a pencil and jotted them down. I could not help smiling at the document when I had completed it. It ran in this way:

Sherlock Holmes—his limits

1. Knowledge of Literature.—Nil.
2. Knowledge of Philosophy.—Nil.
3. Knowledge of Astronomy.—Nil.
4. Knowledge of Politics.—Feeble.
5. Knowledge of Botany.—Variable. Well up in belladonna, opium and poisons generally. Knows nothing of practical gardening.
6. Knowledge of Geology.—Practical, but limited. Tells at a glance different soils from each other. After walks has shown me splashes upon his trousers, and told me by their colour and consistency in what part of London he had received them.
7. Knowledge of Chemistry.—Profound.
8. Knowledge of Anatomy.—Accurate, but unsystematic.
9. Knowledge of Sensational Literature.—Immense. He appears to know every detail of every horror perpetrated in the century.
10. Plays the violin well.
11. Is an expert singlestick player, boxer and swordsman.
12. Has a good practical knowledge of British law.

A Study in Scarlet.

I had already observed that he was as sensitive to flattery on the score of his art as any girl could be of her beauty.—*A Study in Scarlet.*

"If there's a vacant place for a chief of the police, I reckon you are the man for it."—Jefferson Hope, *A Study in Scarlet*.

"Populus me sibilat, at mihi plaudo
Ipse domi simul ac nummos contemplar in arca."

Holmes, *A Study in Scarlet*.

"Which is it today," I asked, "morphine or cocaine?"
He raised his eyes languidly from the old black-letter volume which he had opened.
"It is cocaine," he said, "a seven-per-cent solution. Would you care to try it?"
"May I ask whether you have any professional inquiry on foot at present?"
"None. Hence the cocaine. I cannot live without brain-work. What else is there to live for? Stand at the window here. Was ever such a dreary, dismal, unprofitable world? See how the yellow fog swirls down the street and drifts across the dun-coloured houses. What could be more hopelessly prosaic and material? What is the use of having powers, doctor, when one has no field upon which to exert them?"—*The Sign of Four*.

"You really are an automaton—a calculating machine . . . there is something positively inhuman in you at times."
"It is of the first importance not to allow your judgment to be biased by personal qualities."—*The Sign of Four*.

He was bright, eager, and in excellent spirits, a mood which in his case alternated with fits of the blackest depression.—*The Sign of Four*.

"I don't think you can have forgotten me. Don't you remember the amateur who fought three rounds with

10—s.h.c.

you at Alison's rooms on the night of your benefit four years back?"—Holmes to McMurdo, *The Sign of Four.*

"Not Mr. Sherlock Holmes!" roared the prize-fighter. "God's truth! how could I have mistook you? If instead o' standin' there so quiet you had just stepped up and given me that cross-hit of yours under the jaw, I'd ha' known you without a question. Ah, you're one that has wasted your gifts, you have! You might have aimed high, if you had joined the fancy."—*The Sign of Four.*

He took up his violin from the corner, and as I stretched myself out he began to play some low, dreamy, melodious air—his own, no doubt, for he had a remarkable gift for improvisation. I have a vague remembrance of his gaunt limbs, his earnest face, and the rise and fall of his bow.— *The Sign of Four.*

He would hardly reply to my questions, and busied himself all the evening in an abstruse chemical analysis which involved much heating of retorts and distilling of vapours, ending at last in a smell which fairly drove me out of the apartment.—*The Sign of Four.*

"Ah, you rogue!" cried Jones, highly delighted. "You would have made an actor, and a rare one. You had the proper workhouse cough, and those weak legs of yours are worth ten pounds a week."—*The Sign of Four.*

He spoke on a quick succession of subjects—on miracle plays, on mediaeval pottery, on Stradivarius violins, on the Buddhism of Ceylon, and on the warships of the future— handling each as though he had made a special study of it. —*The Sign of Four.*

"I get a wife out of it, Jones gets the credit; pray what remains for you?"

"For me," said Sherlock Holmes, "there still remains the cocaine-bottle."—*The Sign of Four.*

It was not that he felt any emotion akin to love for Irene Adler. All emotions, and that one particularly, were abhorrent to his cold, precise, but admirably balanced mind. He was, I take it, the most perfect reasoning and observing machine that the world has seen: but, as a lover, he would have placed himself in a false position.—*A Scandal in Bohemia.*

"I know, my dear Watson, that you share my love of all that is bizarre and outside the conventions and hum-drum routine of everyday life."—*The Red-headed League.*

All the afternoon he sat in the stalls wrapped in the most perfect happiness, gently waving his long thin fingers in time to the music, while his gently smiling face and his languid, dreamy eyes were as unlike those of Holmes the sleuth-hound, Holmes the relentless, keen-witted, ready-handed criminal agent, as it was possible to conceive. In his singular character the dual nature alternately asserted itself.—*The Red-headed League.*

Sherlock Holmes was transformed when he was hot upon such a scent as this. Men who had only known the quiet thinker and logician of Baker Street would have failed to recognize him. His face flushed and darkened. His brows were drawn into two hard, black lines, while his eyes shone out from beneath them with a steely glitter. —*The Boscombe Valley Mystery.*

"If I remember rightly, you on one occasion, in the early days of our friendship, defined my limits in a very precise fashion."

"Yes . . . it was a singular document. Philosophy, astronomy, and politics were marked at zero, I remember. Botany variable, geology profound as regards the mud-stains from any region within fifty miles of town, chemistry eccentric, anatomy unsystematic, sensational literature and crime records unique, violin player, boxer, swordsman, lawyer, and self-poisoner by cocaine and tobacco."—*The Five Orange Pips*.

Openshaw: "He said that you could solve anything."
Holmes: "He said too much."
Openshaw: "That you are never beaten."
Holmes: "I have been beaten four times—three times by men and once by a woman."—*The Five Orange Pips*.

It was difficult to refuse any of Sherlock Holmes' requests, for they were always so exceedingly definite, and put forward with such an air of mastery.—*The Man with the Twisted Lip*.

He constructed a sort of Eastern divan, upon which he perched himself cross-legged, with an ounce of shag tobacco and a box of matches laid out in front of him. In the dim light of the lamp I saw him sitting there, an old brier pipe between his lips, his eyes fixed vacantly upon the corner of the ceiling, the blue smoke curling up from him, silent, motionless, with the light shining upon his strong-set aquiline features.—*The Man with the Twisted Lip*.

He was lounging upon the sofa in a purple dressing-gown, a pipe-rack within his reach upon the right. . . . A lens and a forceps lying upon the seat of the chair. . . . *The Blue Carbuncle*.

Working as he did rather for the love of his art than for the acquirement of wealth, he refused to associate himself with any investigation which did not tend towards the unusual, and even the fantastic.—*The Speckled Band.*

I had no keener pleasure than in following Holmes in his professional investigations, and in admiring the rapid deductions, as swift as intuitions, and yet always founded on a logical basis, with which he unravelled the problems which were submitted to him.—*The Speckled Band.*

As he spoke he picked up the steel poker, and with a sudden effort straightened it out again.—*The Speckled Band.*

"Yes . . . my correspondence has certainly the charm of variety, and the humbler are usually the more interesting. This looks like one of those unwelcome social summonses which call upon a man either to be bored or to lie.—*The Noble Bachelor.*

"I assure you, Watson, without affectation, that the status of my client is a matter of less moment to me than the interest of his case."—*The Noble Bachelor.*

"I read nothing except the criminal news and the agony column. The latter is always instructive."—*The Noble Bachelor.*

Sherlock Holmes was a man who seldom took exercise for exercise's sake. Few men were capable of greater muscular effort, and he was undoubtedly one of the finest boxers of his weight that I have ever seen; but he looked upon aimless bodily exertion as a waste of energy, and he seldom bestirred himself save where there was some professional object to be served. That he should have kept himself in training under such circumstances is remarkable, but his diet was usually of the sparest, and his habits were simple to the verge of austerity. Save for the occasional use of cocaine he had no vices, and he only turned to the drug as a protest against the monotony of existence when cases were scanty and the papers uninteresting.—*The Yellow Face*.

I heard a ring at the bell followed by the high, somewhat strident, tones of my old companion's voice.—*The Stockbroker's Clerk*.

"My dear fellow, you know my methods."—*The Stockbroker's Clerk*.

His iron constitution . . . had broken down under the strain of an investigation which had extended over two months, during which period he had never worked less than fifteen hours a day.—*The Reigate Squires*.

"You remember the small affair of Uriah and Bathsheba? My Biblical knowledge is a trifle rusty, I fear, but you will find the story in the first or second of Samuel."—*The Crooked Man*.

He had, when he so willed it, the utter immobility of countenance of a Red Indian.—*The Naval Treaty*.

He had a horror of destroying documents, especially those which were connected with his past cases.—*The Musgrave Ritual*.

His cold and proud nature was always averse, however, to anything in the shape of public applause, and he bound me in the most stringent terms to say no further word of himself, his methods, or his successes.—*The Norwood Builder*.

"I get so little active exercise that it is always a treat. . . . You are aware that I have some proficiency in the good old British sport of boxing. Occasionally it is of service. Today, for example, I should have come to very ignominious grief without it."—*The Solitary Cyclist.*

I have never known my friend to be in better form, both mental and physical, than in the year '95. His increasing fame had brought with it an immense practice, and I should be guilty of an indiscretion if I were even to hint at the identity of some of the illustrious clients who crossed our humble threshold in Baker Street. Holmes, however, like all great artists, lived for his art's sake, and, save in the case of the Duke of Holdernesse, I have seldom known him claim any large reward for his inestimable services.—*Black Peter.*

A flush of colour sprang to Holmes's pale cheeks, and he bowed to us like the master dramatist who receives the homage of his audience. . . . The same singularly proud and reserved nature which turned away with disdain from popular notoriety was capable of being moved to its depths by spontaneous wonder and praise from a friend.—*The Six Napoleons.*

My friend's temper had not improved since he had been deprived of the congenial surroundings of Baker Street. Without his scrap-books, his chemicals, and his homely untidiness, he was an uncomfortable man.—*The Three Students.*

When we rose again I observed that Holmes's eyes were shining and his cheeks tinged with colour. Only at a crisis have I seen those battle-signals flying.—*The Golden Pince-nez.*

For years I had gradually weaned him from that drug mania which had threatened once to check his remarkable career. Now I knew that under ordinary conditions he no longer craved for this artificial stimulus; but I was well aware that the fiend was not dead, but sleeping. . . .—*The Missing Three-quarter*.

"You live in a different world to me, Mr. Overton, a sweeter and healthier one. My ramifications stretch out into many sections of society, but never, I am happy to say, into amateur sport, which is the best and soundest thing in England."—*The Missing Three-quarter*.

Sherlock Holmes was a past master in the art of putting a humble witness at his ease.—*The Missing Three-quarter*.

All that day and the next Holmes was in a mood which his friends would call taciturn, and others morose. He ran out and ran in, smoked incessantly, played snatches on his violin, sank into reveries, devoured sandwiches at irregular hours, and hardly answered the casual questions which I put to him.—*The Second Stain*.

"My mind is like a racing engine, tearing itself to pieces because it is not connected up with the work for which it was built."—*Wisteria Lodge*.

We had a pleasant little meal together, during which Holmes would talk about nothing but violins, narrating with great exultation how he had purchased his own Stradivarius, which was worth at least five hundred guineas, at a Jew broker's in Tottenham Court Road for fifty-five shillings. This led him to Paganini, and we sat for an hour over a bottle of claret while he told me anecdote after anecdote of that extraordinary man.—*The Cardboard Box*.

Holmes was accessible upon the side of flattery, and also, to do him justice, upon the side of kindliness.—*The Red Circle*.

He had an almost hypnotic power of soothing when he wished.—*The Red Circle.*

See the foxhound with hanging ears and drooping tail . . . and compare it with the same hound as, with gleaming eyes and straining muscles, it runs upon a breast-high scent—such was the change in Holmes since the morning. —*The Bruce-Partington Plans.*

One of the most remarkable characteristics of Sherlock Holmes was his power of throwing his brain out of action and switching all his thoughts on to lighter things whenever he had convinced himself that he could no longer work to advantage.—*The Bruce-Partington Plans.*

To his sombre and cynical spirit all popular applause was always abhorrent, and nothing amused him more at the end of a successful case than to hand over the actual exposure to some orthodox official.—*The Devil's Foot.*

Both Holmes and I had a weakness for the Turkish Bath. It was over a smoke in the pleasant lassitude of the drying room that I have found him less reticent and more human than anywhere else.—*The Illustrious Client.*

It was one of the peculiarities of his proud, self-contained nature that, though he docketed any fresh information very quickly and accurately in his brain, he seldom made any acknowledgment to the giver.—*The Sussex Vampire.*

Holmes had spent several days in bed, as was his habit from time to time, but he emerged that morning with a long foolscap document in his hand. . . .—*The Three Garridebs.*

The clear, hard eyes were dimmed for a moment, and the firm lips were shaking. For the one and only time I caught a glimpse of a great heart as well as of a great brain.—*The Three Garridebs.*

I descended to breakfast prepared to find my companion in depressed spirits, for, like all great artists, he was easily impressed by his surroundings.—*Thor Bridge.*

"My professional charges are upon a fixed scale. I do not vary them, save when I remit them altogether."—*Thor Bridge.*

He would talk of nothing but art, of which he had the crudest ideas.—*The Hound of the Baskervilles.*

He had contrived, with that cat-like love of personal cleanliness which was one of his characteristics, that his chin would be as smooth and his linen as perfect as if he were in Baker Street.—*The Hound of the Baskervilles.*

One of Sherlock Holmes's defects—if, indeed, one may call it a defect—was that he was exceedingly loth to communicate his full plans to any other person until the instant of their fulfilment.—*The Hound of the Baskervilles.*

"I have been to Devonshire."
"In spirit?"
"Exactly. My body has remained in this arm-chair; and has, I regret to observe, consumed in my absence two large pots of coffee and an incredible amount of tobacco."
—*The Hound of the Baskervilles*

Holmes took his pipe from his lips and sat up in his chair like an old hound who hears the view-holloa.—*The Devil's Foot.*

It would take me all my time to break it. An ordinary man could not do it.—*The Beryl Coronet.*

HOLMES AND WATSON ON WATSON

"I am lost without my Boswell."—*A Scandal in Bohemia.*

"I know, my dear **Watson**, that you share my love of all that is bizarre and outside the conventions and humdrum routine of everyday life. You have shown your relish for it by the enthusiasm which has prompted you to chronicle, and, if you will excuse my saying so, somewhat to embellish so many of my own little adventures."—*A Scandal in Bohemia.*

"What do you think, Watson? Could your patients spare you for a few hours?"
"I have nothing to do today. My practice is never very absorbing."—*The Red-headed League.*

My experience of camp life in Afghanistan had at least had the effect of making me a prompt and ready traveller.—*The Boscombe Valley Mystery.*

"Now, Watson . . . you'll come with me, won't you?"
"If I can be of use."
"Oh, a trusty comrade is always of use. And a chronicler still more so."—*The Man with the Twisted Lip.*

"You have a grand gift of silence, Watson. It makes you quite invaluable as a companion."—*The Man with the Twisted Lip.*

I keep a bull pup . . . and I object to row, because my nerves are shaken, and I get up at all sorts of ungodly hours, and I am extremely lazy. I have another set of vices when I'm well, but those are the principal ones at present.—*A Study in Scarlet.*

Shortly after my marriage I had bought a connection in the Paddington district. . . . When I purchased it . . . it had sunk from twelve hundred to little more than three hundred a year. I had confidence, however, in my own youth and energy, and was convinced that in a very few years the concern would be as flourishing as ever.—*The Stockbroker's Clerk.*

"My client is outside in a four-wheeler. Can you come at once?"

"In an instant." I scribbled a note to my neighbour, rushed upstairs to explain the matter to my wife, and joined Holmes upon the doorstep.—*The Stockbroker's Clerk.*

"You are the stormy petrel of crime, Watson."—*The Naval Treaty.*

"The practice is quiet . . . and I have an accommodating neighbour. I should be glad to come."—*The Final Problem.*

"I should say that only a clean-shaven man could have smoked this. Why, Watson, even your modest moustache would have been singed."—*The Red Circle.*

Watson has some remarkable characteristics of his own, to which in his modesty he has given small attention amid his exaggerated estimates of my own performances. A confederate . . . to whom each development comes as a perpetual surprise, and to whom the future is always a closed book, is, indeed, an ideal helpmate.—*The Blanched Soldier.*

"Count me in, Holmes. I have nothing to do for a day or two."

"Your morals don't improve, Watson. You have added fibbing to your other vices. You bear every sign of the busy medical man, with calls on him every hour."—*The Mazarin Stone.*

"I can't possibly leave you."

"Yes, you can, Watson. And you will, for you have never failed to play the game. I am sure you will play it to the end."—*The Mazarin Stone.*

"I never get your limits, Watson . . . there are unexplored possibilities about you."—*The Sussex Vampire.*

"Excellent, Watson! Compound of the Busy Bee and Excelsior."—*The Creeping Man.*

"By the way, Watson, you know something of racing?"

"I ought to. I pay for it with about half my wound pension."—*Shoscombe Old Place.*

My constitution has not got over the Afghan campaign yet. I cannot afford to throw any extra strain upon it.—*The Sign of Four.*

In an experience of women which extends over many nations and three separate continents, I have never looked upon a face which gave a clearer promise of a refined and sensitive nature.—*The Sign of Four.*

What was I, an Army surgeon with a weak leg and a weaker banking account, that I should dare to think of such things? She was a unit, a factor—nothing more.—*The Sign of Four.*

I made no remark . . . but sat nursing my wounded leg. I had had a Jezail bullet through it some time before, and though it did not prevent me from walking, it ached wearily at every change of the weather.—*The Sign of Four.*

I served at the fatal battle of Maiwand. There I was struck on the shoulder by a Jezail bullet, which shattered the bone and grazed the subclavian artery.—*A Study in Scarlet.*

I had remained indoors all day, for the weather had taken a sudden turn to rain, with high autumnal winds, and the Jezail bullet which I had brought back in one of my limbs as a relic of my Afghan campaign, throbbed with dull persistence.—*The Noble Bachelor.*

I had neither kith nor kin in England, and was therefore as free as air—or as free as an income of eleven shillings and sixpence a day will permit a man to be.—*A Study in Scarlet.*

I sat stolidly puffing at my pipe and skipping over the pages of Henri Murger's *Vie de Bohème.*—*A Study in Scarlet.*

The rough-and-tumble work in Afghanistan, coming on the top of a natural Bohemianism of disposition, has made me rather more lax than befits a medical man. But with me there is a limit, and when I find a man who keeps his cigars in the coal-scuttle, his tobacco in the toe-end of a Persian slipper, and his unanswered correspondence transfixed by a jack-knife into the very centre of his wooden mantelpiece, then I begin to give myself virtuous airs.— *The Musgrave Ritual.*

"What with your eternal tobacco, Watson, and your irregularity at meals, I expect that you *will* get notice to quit, and that I shall share your downfall."—*The Three Students.*

"There is a delightful freshness about you, Watson, which makes it a pleasure to exercise any small powers which I may possess at your expense."—*The Hound of the Baskervilles*.

"I am inclined to think——" said I.
"I should do so," Sherlock Holmes remarked, impatiently.—*The Valley of Fear*.

"You are developing a certain vein of pawky humour, Watson, against which I must learn to guard myself."—*The Valley of Fear*.

"Your native shrewdness, my dear Watson, that innate cunning which is the delight of your friends, would surely prevent you from enclosing cipher and message in the same envelope."—*The Valley of Fear*.

"Perhaps there are points which have escaped your Machiavellian intellect."—*The Valley of Fear*.

"You have really done very well indeed. It is true that you have missed everything of importance. . . ."—*A Case of Identity*.

HOLMES PHILOSOPHIZES

"My dear fellow, life is infinitely stranger than anything which the mind of man could invent. We would not dare to conceive the things which are really mere commonplaces of existence. If we could fly out of that window hand in hand, hover over this great city, gently remove the roofs, and peep in at the queer things which are going on, the strange coincidences, the plannings, the cross-purposes, the wonderful chain of events, working through generations, and leading to the most *outré* results, it would make all fiction with its conventionalities and foreseen conclusions most stale and unprofitable."—*A Case of Identity*.

"Depend upon it, there is nothing so unnatural as the commonplace."—*A Case of Identity*.

"My life is spent in one long effort to escape from the commonplaces of existence."—*The Red-headed League*.

"God help us! Why does Fate play such tricks with poor helpless worms? I never hear of such a case as this that I do not think of Baxter's words, and say: 'There, but for the grace of God, goes Sherlock Holmes!' "—*The Boscombe Valley Mystery*.

"A man should keep his little brain attic stocked with all the furniture that he is likely to use, and the rest he can put away in the lumber-room of his library, where he can get it if he wants it."—*The Five Orange Pips*.

". . . one of those whimsical little incidents which will happen when you have four million human beings all jostling each other within the space of a few square miles. Amid the action and reaction of so dense a swarm of humanity, every possible combination of events may be expected to take place, and many a little problem will be presented which may be striking and bizarre without being criminal."—*The Blue Carbuncle*.

"I suppose that I am commuting a felony, but it is just possible that I am saving a soul . . . besides, it is the season of forgiveness."—*The Blue Carbuncle*.

Hatherley: "I have lost my thumb, and I have lost a fifty-guinea fee, and what have I gained?"
Holmes: "Experience. Indirectly it may be of value, you know; you have only to put it into words to gain the reputation of being excellent company for the remainder of your existence."—*The Engineer's Thumb*.

"Human nature is a strange mixture, Watson. You see that even a villain and a murderer can inspire such affection that his brother turns to suicide when he learns that his neck is forfeited."—*The Stockbroker's Clerk*.

"There is nothing in which deduction is so necessary as in religion. It can be built up as an exact science by the reasoner. Our highest assurance of the goodness of Providence seems to me to rest in the flowers. All other things, our powers, our desires, our food, are really necessary for our existence in the first instance. But this rose is an extra. Its smell and its colour are an embellishment of life, not a condition of it. It is only goodness which gives extras, and so I say again that we have much to hope from the flowers."—*The Naval Treaty*.

Holmes: "Look at those big, isolated clumps of buildings rising up above the slates, like brick islands in a lead-coloured sea."
Watson: "The Board schools."
Holmes: "Lighthouses, my boy! Beacons of the future! Capsules, with hundreds of bright little seeds in each, out of which will spring the wiser, better England of the future."—*The Naval Treaty*.

"I think that I may go so far as to say, Watson, that I have not lived wholly in vain. If my record were closed tonight I could still survey it with equanimity. The air of London is the sweeter for my presence. In over a thousand cases I am not aware that I have ever used my powers upon the wrong side. Of late I have been tempted to look into the problems furnished by Nature rather than those more superficial ones for which our artificial state of society is responsible."—*The Final Problem*.

"There are some trees, Watson, which grow to a certain height and then suddenly develop some unsightly

11—S.H.C.

eccentricity. You will see it often in humans. I have a theory that the individual represents in his development the whole procession of his ancestors, and that such a sudden turn to good or evil stands for some strong influence which came into the line of his pedigree. The person becomes, as it were, the epitome of the history of his own family."—*The Empty House.*

"Once or twice in my career I feel that I have done more real harm by my discovery of the criminal than ever he had done by his crime. I have learned caution now, and I had rather play tricks with the law of England than with my own conscience."—*The Abbey Grange.*

"What is the meaning of it, Watson? What object is served by this circle of misery and violence and fear? It must tend to some end, or else our universe is ruled by chance, which is unthinkable. But what end? There is the great standing perennial problem to which human reason is as far from an answer as ever."—*The Cardboard Box.*

"We have helped a remarkable woman, and also a formidable man. Should they in the future join their forces, as seems not unlikely, the financial world may find that Mr. Neil Gibson has learned something in the schoolroom of Sorrow where our earthly lessons are taught."—*Thor Bridge.*

"The ways of Fate are indeed hard to understand. If there is not some compensation hereafter, then the world is a cruel jest."—*The Veiled Lodger.*

Holmes: "Your life is not your own. Keep your hands off it."
Eugenia Ronder: "What use is it to anyone?"

Holmes: "How can you tell? The example of patient suffering is in itself the most precious of all lessons to an impatient world."—*The Veiled Lodger*.

"Is not all life pathetic and futile? Is not his story a microcosm of the whole? We reach. We grasp. And what is left in our hands at the end? A shadow. Or worse than a shadow—misery."—*The Retired Colourman*.

"How sweet the morning air is! See how that one little cloud floats like a pink feather from some gigantic flamingo. Now the red rim of the sun pushes itself over the London cloud-bank. It shines on a good many folk, but on none, I dare bet, who are on a stranger errand than you and I. How small we feel, with our petty ambitions and strivings in the presence of the great elemental forces of Nature."—*The Sign of Four*.

"He (Richter) makes one curious but profound remark. It is that the chief proof of man's real greatness lies in his perception of his own smallness. It argues, you see, a power of comparison and of appreciation which is in itself a proof of nobility."—*The Sign of Four*.

"Dirty-looking rascals, but I suppose everyone has some little immortal spark concealed about him. You would not think it to look at them. There is no *a priori* probability about it. A strange enigma is man."—*The Sign of Four*.

"You can . . . never foretell what any one man will do, but you can say with precision what an average number will be up to. Individuals vary, but percentages remain constant."—*The Sign of Four*.

"A client is to me a mere unit, a factor in a problem. The emotional qualities are antagonistic to clear reasoning."—*The Sign of Four*.

"One's ideas must be as broad as Nature if they are to interpret Nature."—*A Study in Scarlet*.

"To a great mind, nothing is little."—*A Study in Scarlet*.

"Where there is no imagination there is no horror."— *A Study in Scarlet*.

"What you do in this world is a matter of no consequence. The question is, what you can make people believe that you have done."—*A Study in Scarlet*.

"Some people without possessing genius have a remarkable power of stimulating it."—*The Hound of the Baskervilles*.

"It is my experience that it is only an amiable man in this world who receives testimonials, only an unambitious one who abandons a London career for the country and only an absent-minded one who leaves his stick and not his visiting-card after waiting an hour in your room."—*The Hound of the Baskervilles*.

"In a modest way I have combated evil, but to take on the Father of Evil himself would, perhaps, be too ambitious a task."—*The Hound of the Baskervilles*.

"When one tries to rise above Nature one is liable to fall below it. The highest type of man may revert to the animal if he leaves the straight road of destiny."—*The Creeping Man*.

"I cannot agree with those who rank modesty among the virtues. To a logician all things should be seen exactly as they are, and to underestimate oneself is as much a departure from truth as to exaggerate one's own powers." —*The Greek Interpreter*.

"To let the brain work without sufficient material is like racing an engine. It racks itself to pieces. The sea air, sunshine and patience, Watson—all else will come."—*The Devil's Foot.*

"The world is big enough for us. No ghosts need apply."—*The Sussex Vampire.*

ON DETECTION AND CRIME

"If a gentleman walks into my rooms smelling of iodoform, with a black mark of nitrate of silver upon his right forefinger, and a bulge on the side of his top hat to show where he has secreted his stethoscope, I must be dull indeed if I do not pronounce him to be an active member of the medical profession."—*A Scandal in Bohemia.*

"It is a capital mistake to theorize before one has data. Insensibly one begins to twist facts to suit theories, instead of theories to suit facts."—*A Scandal in Bohemia.*

"As a rule, when I have heard some slight indication of the course of events I am able to guide myself by the thousands of other similar cases which occur to my memory."—*The Red-headed League.*

"The strangest and most unique things are very often connected not with the larger but with the smaller crimes, and occasionally, indeed, where there is room for doubt whether any positive crime has been committed."—*The Red-headed League.*

"Beyond the obvious facts that he has at some time done manual labour, that he takes snuff, that he is a

Freemason, that he has been in China, and that he has done a considerable amount of writing lately, I can deduce nothing else."—*The Red-headed League*.

"It is usually in unimportant matters that there is a field for observation, and for the quick analysis of cause and effect which gives the charm to an investigation. The larger crimes are apt to be the simpler, for the bigger the crime, the more obvious, as a rule, is the motive."—*A Case of Identity*.

"It is my business to know things. Perhaps I have trained myself to see what others overlook."—*A Case of Identity*.

"It has long been an axiom of mine that the little things are infinitely the most important."—*A Case of Identity*.

"I can never bring you to realize the importance of sleeves, the suggestiveness of thumb-nails, or the great issues that may hang from a bootlace."—*A Case of Identity*.

"Never trust to general impressions, my boy, but concentrate yourself upon details. My first glance is always at a woman's sleeve. In a man it is perhaps better first to take the knee of the trouser."—*A Case of Identity*.

"I think of writing another little monograph some of these days on the typewriter and its relation to crime. It is a subject to which I have devoted some little attention."—*A Case of Identity*.

"Singularity is almost invariably a clue. The more featureless and commonplace a crime is, the more difficult is it to bring it home."—*The Boscombe Valley Mystery*.

"Circumstantial evidence is a very tricky thing; it may seem to point very straight to one thing, but if you shift your own point of view a little, you may find it pointing in an equally uncompromising manner to something entirely different."—*The Boscombe Valley Mystery*.

"You know my method. It is founded upon the observance of trifles."—*The Boscombe Valley Mystery*.

"The ideal reasoner would, when he has once been shown a single fact in all its bearings, deduce from it not only all the chain of events which led up to it, but also all the results which would follow from it. As Cuvier could correctly describe a whole animal by the contemplation of a single bone, so the observer who has thoroughly understood one link in a series of incidents, should be able accurately to state all the other ones, both before and after. We have not yet grasped the results which the reason alone can attain to."—*The Five Orange Pips*.

"What can you gather from this old battered felt?"
"Here is my lens. You know my methods."
"I can see nothing."
"On the contrary, Watson, you can see everything. You fail, however, to reason from what you see. You are too timid in drawing your inferences."—*The Blue Carbuncle*.

"Just see how it glints and sparkles. Of course it is a nucleus and focus of crime. Every good stone is. They are the devil's pet baits. In the larger and older jewels every facet may stand for a bloody deed."—*The Blue Carbuncle*.

"It is always awkward doing business with an alias."—*The Blue Carbuncle*.

"After all, Watson, I am not retained by the police to supply their deficiencies."—*The Blue Carbuncle*.

Holmes: "You have come in by train this morning, I see."

Helen Stoner: "You know me, then?"

Holmes: "No, but I observe the second half of a return ticket in the palm of your left glove."—*The Speckled Band.*

"When a doctor does go wrong he is the first of criminals. He has nerve and he has knowledge. Palmer and Pritchard were among the heads of their profession.—" *The Speckled Band.*

"I had come to an entirely erroneous conclusion, which shows, my dear Watson, how dangerous it always is to reason from insufficient data."—*The Speckled Band.*

"Circumstantial evidence is occasionally very convincing, as when you find a trout in the milk, to quote Thoreau's example."—*The Noble Bachelor.*

"It is an old maxim of mine that when you have excluded the impossible, whatever remains, however improbable, must be the truth."—*The Beryl Coronet.*

"You have given prominence not so much to the many *causes célèbres* and sensational trials in which I have figured, but rather to those incidents which may have been trivial in themselves, but which have given room for those faculties of deduction and of logical synthesis which I have made my special province."—*The Copper Beeches.*

"Crime is common. Logic is rare. Therefore it is upon the logic rather than upon the crime that you should dwell."—*The Copper Beeches.*

"The days of the great cases are past. Man, or at least criminal man, has lost all enterprise and originality. As to my own little practice, it seems to be degenerating into an agency for recovering lost lead pencils and giving advice to young ladies from boarding-schools."—*The Copper Beeches*.

"It is my belief, Watson, founded upon my experience, that the lowest and vilest alleys in London do not present a more dreadful record of sin than does the smiling and beautiful countryside . . . the pressure of public opinion can do in the town what the law cannot accomplish. There is no lane so vile that the scream of a tortured child, or the thud of a drunkard's blow, does not beget sympathy and indignation among the neighbours, and then the whole machinery of justice is ever so close that a word of complaint can set it going, and there is but a step between the crime and the dock. But look at these lonely houses, each in its own fields, filled for the most part with poor ignorant folk who know little of the law. Think of the deeds of hellish cruelty, the hidden wickedness which may go on, year in, year out, in such places, and none the wiser."—*The Copper Beeches*.

"My dear Watson, you as a medical man are continually gaining light as to the tendencies of a child by the study of the parents. Don't you see that the converse is equally valid. I have frequently gained my first real insight into the character of parents by studying their children."—*The Copper Beeches*.

"It has always been my habit to hide none of my methods, either from my friend Watson or from anyone who might take an intelligent interest in them."—*The Reigate Squires*.

"You may not be aware that the deduction of a man's age from his writing is one which has been brought to considerable accuracy by experts."—*The Reigate Squires*.

"Elementary. It is one of those instances when the reasoner can produce an effect which seems remarkable to his neighbour, because the latter has missed the one little point which is the basis of the deduction."—*The Crooked Man.*

"You come at a crisis, Watson. If this paper remains blue, all is well. If it turns red, it means a man's life."—*The Naval Treaty.*

Holmes: "I clambered over the fence into the grounds."
Phelps: "Surely the gate was open?"
Holmes: "Yes, but I have a peculiar taste in these matters."—*The Naval Treaty.*

"There is no one who knows the higher criminal world of London so well as I do. For years past I have continually been conscious of some power behind the malefactor, some deep organizing power which for ever stands in the way of the law, and throws its shield over the wrong-doer."—*The Final Problem.*

"From the point of view of the criminal expert London has become a singularly uninteresting city since the death of the late lamented Professor Moriarty . . . the community is certainly the gainer, and no one the loser, save the poor out-of-work specialist, whose occupation has gone. With that man in the field one's morning paper presented infinite possibilities."—*The Norwood Builder.*

"Your neighbour is a doctor?"
"Yes. He bought a practice, as I did."
"An old-established one?"
"Just the same as mine. Both have been ever since the houses were built."
"Ah, then you got hold of the better of the two."

"I think I did. But how do you know?"

"By the steps, my boy. Yours are worn three inches deeper than his."—*The Stockbroker's Clerk.*

"The faculty of deduction is certainly contagious, Watson."—*Thor Bridge.*

"I can discover facts, Watson, but I cannot change them."—*Thor Bridge.*

"It is not really difficult to construct a series of inferences, each dependent upon its predecessor and each simple in itself. If, after doing so, one simply knocks out all the central inferences and presents one's audience with the starting-point and the conclusion, one may produce a startling, though possibly a meretricious, effect."—*The Dancing Men.*

"Every problem becomes very childish when once it is explained to you."—*The Dancing Men.*

"I am fairly familiar with all forms of secret writings, and am myself the author of a trifling monograph upon the subject, in which I analyse one hundred and sixty separate ciphers; but I confess that this is entirely new to me."—*The Dancing Men.*

"A bicycle certainly, but not *the* bicycle. I am familiar with forty-two different impressions left by tyres."—*The Priory School.*

"One should always look for a possible alternative and provide against it. It is the first rule of criminal investigation."—*Black Peter.*

"I would ask you how could one compare the ruffian who in hot blood bludgeons his mate, with this man, who methodically and at his leisure tortures the soul and wrings the nerves in order to add to his already swollen money-bags?"—*Charles Augustus Milverton.*

"You know, Watson, I don't mind confessing to you that I have always had an idea that I would have made a highly efficient criminal . . . see here! This is a first-class, up-to-date burgling kit, with nickel-plated jemmy, diamond-tipped glass cutter, adaptable keys, and every modern improvement which the march of civilisation demands."—*Charles Augustus Milverton.*

"I think there are certain crimes which the law cannot touch, and which therefore, to some extent, justify private revenge."—*Charles Augustus Milverton.*

"I propose to devote my declining years to the composition of a textbook which shall focus the whole art of detection into one volume."—*The Abbey Grange.*

"Perhaps when a man has special knowledge and special powers like my own it rather encourages him to seek a complex explanation when a simpler one is at hand."—*The Abbey Grange*

"You will remember, Watson, how the dreadful business of the Abernetty family was first brought to my notice by the depth which the parsley had sunk into the butter on a hot day."—*The Six Napoleons.*

"I choose to be only associated with those crimes which present some difficulty in their solution."—*The Cardboard Box.*

"Look out of this window, Watson. See how the figures loom up, are dimly seen, and then blend once more into the cloud-bank. The thief or the murderer could roam

London on such a day as the tiger does the jungle, unseen until he pounces, and then evident only to his victim."— *The Bruce-Partington Plans.*

"It is fortunate for this community that I am not a criminal. . . . Suppose that I were Brooks or Woodhouse, or any of the fifty men who have good reason for taking my life, how long could I survive against my own pursuit? A summons, a bogus appointment, and all would be over. It is well they don't have days of fog in the Latin countries —the countries of assassination."—*The Bruce-Partington Plans.*

"When you follow two separate chains of thought, Watson, you will find some point of intersection which should approximate to the truth."—*The Disappearance of Lady Frances Carfax.*

"A complex mind—all great criminals have that. My old friend Charlie Peace was a violin virtuoso. Wainwright was no mean artist."—*The Illustrious Client.*

"I have been down to see friend Lestrade at the Yard. There may be an occasional want of imaginative intuition down there, but they lead the world for thoroughness and method."—*The Three Garridebs.*

"How often have I said to you that when you have eliminated the impossible, whatever remains, however improbable, must be the truth?"—*The Sign of Four.*

"I never make exceptions. An exception disproves the rule."—*The Sign of Four.*

"Like all other arts, the Science of Deduction and Analysis is one which can only be acquired by long and

patient study, nor is life long enough to allow any mortal
to attain the highest possible perfection in it."—*The Sign
of Four*.

"By a man's finger-nails, by his coat-sleeve, by his boot,
by his trouser-knees, by the callosities of his forefinger
and thumb, by his expression, by his shirt-cuffs—by each
of these things a man's calling is plainly revealed."—*The
Sign of Four*.

"I am the last and highest court of appeal in detection."
—*The Sign of Four*.

"Detection is, or ought to be, an exact science, and
should be treated in the same cold and unemotional
manner. You have attempted to tinge it with romanticism,
which produces much the same effect as if you worked a
love-story or an elopement into the fifth proposition of
Euclid."—*The Sign of Four*.

"No doubt you think that you are complimenting me in
comparing me to Dupin. Now, in my opinion, Dupin was
a very inferior fellow . . . he had some analytical genius,
no doubt; but he was by no means such a phenomenon as
Poe appeared to imagine."—*A Study in Scarlet*.

"Lecoq was a miserable bungler—he had only one
thing to recommend him, and that was his energy."—*A
Study in Scarlet*.

"There are no crimes and no criminals in these days.
What is the use of having brains in our profession? I know
well that I have it in me to make my name famous. No man
lives or has ever lived who has brought the same amount
of study and of natural talent to the detection of crime
which I have done. And what is the result? There is no

crime to detect, or at most, some bungling villainy with a motive so transparent that even a Scotland Yard official can see through it."—*A Study in Scarlet*.

"They say that genius is an infinite capacity for taking pains. It's a very bad definition, but it does apply to detective work."—*A Study in Scarlet*.

"When a fact appears to be opposed to a long train of deductions it invariably proves to be capable of bearing some other interpretation."—*A Study in Scarlet*.

"It is a capital mistake to theorize before you have all the evidence."—*A Study in Scarlet*.

"It is a mistake to confound strangeness with mystery. The most commonplace crime is often the most mysterious, because it presents no new or special features from which deductions may be drawn."—*A Study in Scarlet*.

"In solving a problem of this sort, the grand thing is to be able to reason backwards. That is a very useful accomplishment, and a very easy one, but people do not practise it much. In the everyday affairs of life it is more useful to reason forwards, and so the other comes to be neglected. There are fifty who can reason synthetically for one who can reason analytically."—*A Study in Scarlet*.

"There's the scarlet thread of murder running through the colourless skein of life, and our duty is to unravel it, and isolate it, and expose every inch of it."—*A Study in Scarlet*.

"There is no branch of detective science which is so important and so much neglected as the art of tracing footsteps."—*A Study in Scarlet*.

"The world is full of obvious things which nobody by any chance ever observes."—*The Hound of the Baskervilles*.

"The detection of types is one of the most elementary branches of knowledge to the special expert in crime, though I confess that once when I was very young I confused the *Leeds Mercury* with the *Western Morning News*." —*The Hound of the Baskervilles*.

"There is nothing more stimulating than a case where everything goes against you."—*The Hound of the Baskervilles*.

"My eyes have been trained to examine faces and not their trimmings. It is the first quality of a criminal investigator that he should see through a disguise."—*The Hound of the Baskervilles*.

"There are seventy-five perfumes, which it is very necessary that a criminal expert should be able to distinguish from each other."—*The Hound of the Baskervilles*.

"Surely our profession . . . would be a drab and sordid one if we did not sometimes set the scene so as to glorify our results. The blunt accusation, the brutal tap upon the shoulder—what can one make of such a denouement? But the quick inference, the subtle trap, the clever forecast of coming events, the triumphant vindication of bold theories —are these not the pride and the justification of our life's work?"—*The Valley of Fear*.

"If criminals would always schedule their movements like railway trains it would certainly be more convenient for all of us."—*The Valley of Fear*.

"You can tell an old master by the sweep of his brush. I can tell a Moriarty when I see one. . . ."—*The Valley of Fear*.

Inspector Gregory: "Is there any other point to which you would wish to draw my attention?"

Holmes: "To the curious incident of the dog in the night-time."

Inspector Gregory: "The dog did nothing in the night-time."

Holmes: "That was the curious incident."—*Silver Blaze*.

Holmes: "I followed you."

Sterndale: "I saw no one."

Holmes: "That is what you may expect to see when I follow you."—*The Devil's Foot*.

ON WOMEN

"Women are naturally secretive, and they like to do their own secreting."—*A Scandal in Bohemia*.

"When a woman thinks that her house is on fire, her instinct is at once to rush to the thing which she values most. It is a perfectly overpowering impulse, and I have more than once taken advantage of it. . . . A married woman grabs at her baby—an unmarried one reaches for her jewel box."—*A Scandal in Bohemia*.

"Oscillation upon the pavement always means an *affaire du cœur*. She would like advice, but is not sure that the matter is not too delicate for communication. And yet even here we may discriminate. When a woman has been seriously wronged by a man she no longer oscillates, and the usual symptom is a broken bell wire."—*A Case of Identity*.

"You may remember the old Persian saying, 'There is danger for him who taketh the tiger cub, and danger also

12—S.H.C.

for whoso snatches a delusion from a woman.' There is as much sense in Hafiz as in Horace, and as much knowledge of the world."—*A Case of Identity.*

"I have seen too much not to know that the impression of a woman may be more valuable than the conclusion of an analytical reasoner."—*The Man with the Twisted Lip.*

"Ah! Watson, perhaps you would not be very gracious either, if, after all the trouble of wooing and wedding, you found yourself deprived in an instant of wife and fortune." —*The Noble Bachelor.*

"There are women in whom the love of a lover extinguishes all other loves."—*The Beryl Coronet.*

"A man always finds it hard to realize that he may have finally lost a woman's love, however badly he may have treated her."—*The Musgrave Ritual.*

"She . . . had flown to tea, as an agitated woman will." —*The Crooked Man.*

"It is part of the settled order of Nature that such a girl should have followers, but for choice not on bicycles in lonely country roads."—*The Solitary Cyclist.*

"It is a pity he did not write in pencil. As you have no doubt frequently observed, Watson, the impression usually goes through—a fact which has dissolved many a happy marriage."—*The Missing Three-quarter.*

"The motives of women are so inscrutable. You remember the woman at Margate whom I suspected for the same reason. No powder on her nose—that proved to be the correct solution. How can you build on such a quicksand? Their most trivial action may mean volumes, or their most extraordinary conduct may depend upon a hairpin or a curling-tongs."—*The Second Stain*.

"One of the most dangerous classes in the world is the drifting and friendless woman. She is the most harmless, and often the most useful of mortals, but she is the inevitable inciter of crime in others. She is helpless. She is migratory. She has sufficient means to take her from country to country and from hotel to hotel. She is lost, as often as not, in a maze of obscure *pensions* and boarding-houses. She is a stray chicken in a world of foxes. When she is gobbled up she is hardly missed."—*The Disappearance of Lady Frances Carfax*.

"I have never loved, Watson, but if I did and if the woman I loved had met such an end, I might act even as our lawless lion-hunter has done."—*The Devil's Foot*.

"Woman's heart and mind are insoluble puzzles to the male. Murder might be condoned or explained, and yet some smaller offence might rankle."—*The Illustrious Client*.

"I pictured to her the awful position of the woman who only wakes to a man's character after she is his wife—a woman who has to submit to be caressed by bloody hands and lecherous lips."—*The Illustrious Client*.

"I thought of her for the moment as I would have thought of a daughter of my own."—*The Illustrious Client*.

"Women have seldom been an attraction to me, for my brain has always governed my heart; but I could not look upon her perfect clear-cut face, with all the soft freshness of the Downlands in her delicate colouring, without realizing that no young man would cross her path unscathed."—*The Lion's Mane*.

"I assure you that the most winning woman I ever knew was hanged for poisoning three little children for their insurance-money."—*The Sign of Four*.

"Women are never to be entirely trusted—not the best of them."—*The Sign of Four*.

"Love is an emotional thing, and whatever is emotional is opposed to that true, cold reason which I place above all things. I should never marry myself, lest I bias my judgment."—*The Sign of Four*.

"I am not a whole-souled admirer of womankind, as you are aware, Watson, but my experience of life has taught me that there are few wives having any regard for their husbands who would let any man's spoken word stand between them and that husband's dead body. Should I ever marry, Watson, I should hope to inspire my wife with some feeling which would prevent her from being walked off by a housekeeper when my corpse was lying within a few yards of her. . . . Even the rawest of investigators must be struck by the absence of the usual feminine ululation."—*The Valley of Fear*.

"No woman would ever send a reply-paid telegram. She would have come."—*Wisteria Lodge*.

ON FOOD, DRINK AND HOSTELRIES

He walked up to the sideboard, and, tearing a piece from the loaf, he devoured it voraciously, washing it down with a long draught of water.

"You are hungry," I remarked.—*The Five Orange Pips*.

"I am somewhat of a fowl fancier, and I have seldom seen a better-grown goose."—*The Blue Carbuncle*.

"Your beer should be excellent if it is as good as your geese."—*The Blue Carbuncle*.

"If you will have the goodness to touch the bell, Doctor, we will begin another investigation, in which also a bird will be the chief feature."—*The Blue Carbuncle*.

A quite epicurean little cold supper began to be laid out upon our humble lodging-house mahogany. There were a couple of brace of cold woodcock, a pheasant, a *pâté-de-foie-gras* pie, with a group of ancient and cobwebby bottles.—*The Noble Bachelor*.

"Mrs. Hudson has risen to the occasion. Her cuisine is a little limited, but she has as good an idea of breakfast as a Scotchwoman. What have you there, Watson?"

"Ham and eggs."

"Good! What are you going to take, Mr. Phelps: curried fowl, eggs, or will you help yourself?"

"Thank you, I can eat nothing."

"Oh, come! Try the dish before you."—*The Naval Treaty*.

"The doctor has a prescription containing hot water and a lemon which is good medicine on a night like this."—*The Golden Pince-nez*.

"Am dining at Goldini's Restaurant, Gloucester Road, Kensington. Please come at once and join me there. Bring with you a jemmy, a dark lantern, a chisel and a revolver."—*The Bruce-Partington Plans*.

"It is a good wine, Holmes."

"A remarkable wine, Watson. Our friend upon the sofa

has assured me that it is from Franz Joseph's special cellar at the Schoenbrunn Palace. Might I trouble you to open the window, for chloroform vapour does not help the palate."—*His Last Bow.*

"We may discuss it when you have consumed the two hard-boiled eggs with which our new cook has favoured us. Their condition may not be unconnected with the copy of the *Family Herald* which I observed yesterday upon the hall-table. Even so trivial a matter as cooking an egg demands an attention which is conscious of the passage of time, and incompatible with the love romance in that excellent periodical."—*Thor Bridge.*

"There is a cold partridge on the sideboard, Watson, and a bottle of Montrachet. Let us renew our energies before we make a fresh call upon them."—*The Veiled Lodger.*

"I insist upon your dining with us. It will be ready in half an hour. I have oysters and a brace of grouse, with something a little choice in white wines. Watson, you have never yet recognized my merits as a housekeeper."—*The Sign of Four.*

He cut a slice of beef from the joint upon the sideboard, sandwiched it between two rounds of bread, and, thrusting this rude meal into his pocket, he started off upon his expedition.—*The Beryl Coronet.*

"Tomorrow, Mr. Bennett, will certainly see us in Camford. There is, if I remember right, an inn called the 'Chequers' where the port used to be above mediocrity, and the linen was above reproach. I think, Watson, that our lot for the next few days might lie in less pleasant places."—*The Creeping Man.*

"I much fear, my dear Watson, that there is no return train tonight. I have unwittingly condemned you to the horrors of a country inn."—*The Retired Colourman*.

"You remember the little chap at the Express office . . . he has seen after my simple wants: a loaf of bread and a clean collar. What does man want more?"—*The Hound of the Baskervilles*.

"Within a week he had settled his bill at one of the most select London hotels."
"How did you deduce the select?"
"By the select prices. Eight shillings for a bed and eightpence for a glass of sherry, pointed to one of the most expensive hotels. There are not many in London which charge at that rate."—*The Noble Bachelor*.

"The sofa is very much superior to the usual country hotel abomination."—*The Boscombe Valley Mystery*.

"But we may be comfortable in the meantime, may we not? Is alcohol permitted? The gasogene and cigars are in the old place. Let me see you once more in the customary armchair."—*The Mazarin Stone*.

Mrs. Hudson: "When will you be pleased to dine, Mr. Holmes?"
Holmes: "Seven-thirty, the day after tomorrow."—*The Mazarin Stone*.

"By Jove! my dear fellow, it is nearly nine, and the landlady babbled of green peas at seven-thirty."—*The Three Students*.

"My dear Watson, when I have exterminated that fourth egg I will be ready to put you in touch with the whole situation."—*The Valley of Fear*.

ON TOBACCO

"It is quite a three-pipe problem, and I beg that you won't speak to me for fifty minutes."—*The Red-headed League*.

"I found the ash of a cigar, which my special knowledge of tobacco ashes enabled me to pronounce as an Indian cigar. I have, as you know, devoted some attention to this, and written a little monograph on the ashes of 140 different varieties of pipe, cigar, and cigarette tobacco."—*The Boscombe Valley Mystery*.

"Halloa! that's not your pipe on the table! He must have left his behind him. A nice old briar, with a good long stem of what the tobacconists call amber. I wonder how many real amber mouthpieces there are in London. Some people think a fly in it is a sign. Why, it is quite a branch of trade, the putting of sham flies into the sham amber."—*The Yellow Face*.

"It has, you see, been twice mended: once in the wooden stem and once in the amber. Each of these mends, done, as you observe, with silver bands, must have cost more than the pipe did originally."—*The Yellow Face*.

"Pipes are occasionally of extraordinary interest. Nothing has more individuality save, perhaps, watches and bootlaces."—*The Yellow Face*.

"This is Grosvenor mixture at eightpence an ounce. As he might get an excellent smoke for half the price, he has no need to practise economy."—*The Yellow Face*.

Sherlock Holmes . . . was smoking his before-breakfast pipe, which was composed of all the plugs and dottles left from his smokes of the day before, all carefully dried and collected on the corner of the mantelpiece.—*The Engineer's Thumb*.

Bradstreet: "I wish I knew how you reach your results." *Holmes*: "I reached this one by sitting upon five pillows and consuming an ounce of shag."—*The Man with the Twisted Lip*.

"Hum! you still smoke the Arcadia mixture of your bachelor days, then! There's no mistaking that fluffy ash upon your coat."—*The Crooked Man*.

"This is a Havana, and these others are cigars of the peculiar sort which are imported by the Dutch from their East India colonies. They are usually wrapped in straw, you know, and are thinner for their length than any other brand. . . . Two have been cut by a not very sharp knife, and two have had the ends bitten off by a set of excellent teeth. This is no suicide, Mr. Lanner. It is a very deeply planned and cold-blooded murder."—*The Resident Patient*.

Mrs. Marker: "His health—well, I don't know that it's better nor worse for the smoking." *Holmes*: "Ah! But it kills the appetite."—*The Golden Pince-nez*.

"I have a caseful of cigarettes here which need smoking." —*The Boscombe Valley Mystery*.

"You have not, I hope, learned to despise my pipe and my lamentable tobacco? It has to take the place of food these days."

"But why not eat?"

"Because the faculties become refined when you starve

them. Why, surely, as a doctor, my dear Watson, you must admit that what your digestion gains in the way of blood supply is so much lost to the brain."—*The Mazarin Stone*.

"I have been guilty of several monographs. They are all upon technical subjects. Here, for example, is one 'Upon the Distinction Between the Ashes of the Various Tobaccos'. In it I enumerate a hundred and forty forms of cigar, cigarette, and pipe tobacco, with coloured plates illustrating the difference in the ash. It is a point which is continually turning up in criminal trials, and which is sometimes of supreme importance as a clue. If you can say, definitely, for example, that some murder had been done by a man who was smoking an Indian Lunkah, it obviously narrows your field of search. To the trained eye there is as much difference between the black ash of a Trichinopoly and the white fluff of bird's-eye as there is between a cabbage and a potato."—*The Sign of Four*.

"Mrs. Merrilow does not object to tobacco, Watson, if you wish to indulge your filthy habits."—*The Veiled Lodger*.

ON NATURE AND ANIMALS

"The horse is a very gregarious creature."—*Silver Blaze*.

"Our highest assurance of the goodness of Providence seems to me to rest in the flowers."—*The Naval Treaty*.

Violet Smith: "Yes, Mr. Holmes, I teach music."
Holmes: "In the country, I presume, from your complexion."

Violet Smith: "Yes, sir; near Farnham, on the borders of Surrey."

Holmes: "A beautiful neighbourhood, and full of the most interesting associations. You remember, Watson, that it was near there that we took Archie Stamford, the forger."—*The Solitary Cyclist*.

"Let us walk in these beautiful woods, Watson, and give a few hours to the birds and the flowers."—*Black Peter*.

"I'm sure, Watson, a week in the country will be invaluable to you. It is very pleasant to see the first green shoots upon the hedges and the catkins on the hazels once again. With a spud, a tin box, and an elementary book on botany, there are instructive days to be spent."—*Wisteria Lodge*.

"Let me introduce you to Pompey. Pompey is the pride of the local draghounds, no very great flier, as his build will show, but a staunch hound on a scent. . . . Now, boy, come along, and show what you can do."—*The Missing Three-quarter*.

"A dog reflects the family life. Whoever saw a frisky dog in a gloomy family, or a sad dog in a happy one? Snarling people have snarling dogs, dangerous people have dangerous ones."—*The Creeping Man*.

"That the dog should die was after the beautiful, faithful nature of dogs. . . . I saw the faithful little creature, an Airedale terrier, laid out upon the mat in the hall."—*The Lion's Mane*.

"*Cyanea Capillata* is the miscreant's full name, and he can be as dangerous to life as, and far more painful than, the bite of the cobra."—*The Lion's Mane*.

"That was a most beautiful spaniel that was whining in the hall. . . . I am a dog-fancier myself."—*Shoscombe Old Place*.

"Dogs don't make mistakes."—*Shoscombe Old Place*.

"A queer mongrel, with a most amazing power of scent. I would rather have Toby's help than that of the whole detective force in London."—*The Sign of Four*.

ON MUSIC, LITERATURE AND ART

"Sarasate plays at the St. James's Hall this afternoon. What do you think, Watson? Could your patients spare you for a few hours? . . . I observe that there is a good deal of German music on the programme, which is rather more to my taste than Italian or French. It is introspective, and I want to introspect."—*The Red-headed League*.

". . . off to violin-land, where all is sweetness, and delicacy, and harmony."—*The Red-headed League*.

"Hand me over my violin and let us try to forget for half an hour the miserable weather, and the still more miserable ways of our fellow-men."—*The Five Orange Pips*.

"Draw your chair up, and hand me my violin, for the only problem which we have still to solve is how to while away these bleak autumnal evenings."—*The Noble Bachelor*.

"To the man who loves art for its own sake, it is frequently in its least important and lowliest manifestations that the keenest pleasure is to be derived."—*The Copper Beeches*.

"Let it play! These modern gramophones are a remarkable invention."—*The Mazarin Stone*.

"Let us escape from this weary workaday world by the side door of music. Carina sings tonight at the Albert Hall, and we still have time to dress, dine, and enjoy."—*The Retired Colourman*.

"And now for lunch, and then for Norman Neruda. Her attack and her bowing are splendid. What's that little thing of Chopin's she plays so magnificently: Tra-la-la-lira-lira-lay."—*A Study in Scarlet*.

"Do you remember what Darwin says about music? He claims that the power of producing and appreciating it existed among the human race long before the power of speech was arrived at. Perhaps that is why we are so subtly influenced by it. There are vague memories in our souls of those misty centuries when the world was in its childhood."—*A Study in Scarlet*.

"I have a box for *Les Huguenots*. Have you heard the De Reszkes?"—*The Hound of the Baskervilles*.

"Watson won't allow that I know anything of art, but that is mere jealousy, because our views upon the subject differ. Now, these are a really very fine series of portraits. . . . I know what is good when I see it, and I see it now. That's a Kneller, I'll swear, that lady in the blue silk over yonder, and the stout gentleman with the wig ought to be Reynolds."—*The Hound of the Baskervilles*.

"A study of family portraits is enough to convert a man to the doctrine of reincarnation."—*The Hound of the Baskervilles*.

"*The Times* is a paper which is seldom found in any hands but those of the highly educated."—*The Hound of the Baskervilles*.

"The vocabulary of *Bradshaw* is nervous and terse, but limited."—*The Valley of Fear*.

"Though reserved in its earlier vocabulary, it (*Whitaker's Almanack*) becomes, if I remember right, quite garrulous towards the end."—*The Valley of Fear*.

"There is a spirituality about the face . . . which the typewriter does not generate. This lady is a musician."—*The Solitary Cyclist*.

"My turn that way is in my veins, and may have come with my grandmother, who was the sister of Vernet, the French artist. Art in the blood is liable to take the strangest forms."—*The Greek Interpreter*.

He took down the great book in which, day by day, he filed the agony columns of the various London journals. "Dear me!" said he turning over the pages, "what a chorus of groans, cries, and bleatings! What a rag-bag of singular happenings! But surely the most valuable hunting-ground that ever was given to a student of the unusual."—*The Red Circle*.

"The Press, Watson, is a most valuable institution, if you only know how to use it."—*The Six Napoleons*.

MR. HOLMES AND DR. WATSON

'Holmes gave me a sketch of the events'

Silver Blaze

What do we know of Holmes and Watson? Much and little. Much, from each man's self-revelation and the picture of each man seen through the other's eyes. Little, from the actual biographical details in existence about them. Partly this may be put down to their admirable lack of egocentricity—it is your egoist who flies to auto-biography—and partly to lack of foresight in their relatives. What an eternal pity it is that the progenitors of such men are not descended upon by some angel of prophecy, to inform them that the featureless cherub in the cot is marked down for fame! Their early years, like those of Shakespeare, are wrapt in mystery and speculation.

But some things we know, beyond guesswork, of those times before the formation of the greatest partnership in literary history. It was on a summer evening, after tea, when Holmes first began to talk about himself to Watson. Perhaps a shaft of evening sunshine laid its fingers along a flock-papered wall in that famous parlour at 221B, Baker Street. But its beckoning was not sufficiently alluring to tempt the two friends out for a walk in the Park. Over the yet uncleared tea-things (for Mrs. Hudson would be tactful enough to disturb her lodgers as little as possible):

The conversation, which had roamed in a desultory, spasmodic fashion from golf clubs to the causes of the change in the obliquity of the ecliptic, came round at last to the question of atavism and hereditary aptitudes. The point under discussion was how far any singular gift in an individual was due to his ancestry, and how far to his own early training.

This led Watson on to the speculation that Holmes's faculty of observation and peculiar facility for deduction were due to his own systematic training. "To some extent," replied Holmes thoughtfully.

My ancestors were country squires, who appear to have led much the same life as is natural to their class. But, none the less, my turn that way is in my veins, and may have come with my grandmother, who was the sister of Vernet, the French artist. Art in the blood is liable to take the strangest forms.

The conversation then turned upon Holmes's brother Mycroft, who, Holmes remarked, possessed the faculty of observation and facility in deduction to an even larger degree than Sherlock himself. By this time it was six o'clock—a good time, Holmes suggested, for them to visit his remarkable brother at the Diogenes Club—"the queerest club in London".

So we shall never know whether Holmes told Watson any more about his origins: the rest is silence. It seems probable that the country squires dwelt in Sussex, as he chose this county for his retirement, and it is often the case with great town-dwellers that when they leave Town for ever, they revert instinctively to that piece of the country which was their first vision of the Pastoral. It was so with Dickens, identified for ever with London yet secretly loathing its dirt and squalor; he retired to and died in that house at Gadshill which he had wistfully coveted in boyhood. Holmes, in popular imagination, is permanently rooted in Baker Street, where, says Watson,

> he loved to lie in the very centre of five millions of people, with his filaments stretching out and running through them, responsive to every little rumour or suspicion of unsolved crime.

With his own sublime lack of perception, Watson goes on to observe that

> Appreciation of nature found no place among his many gifts, and his only change was when he turned his mind from the evil-doer of the town to track down his brother of the country.

Perhaps Watson was unduly impressed by Holmes's celebrated views on the incidence of crime in cottages. At any rate, he may well have raised his eyebrows at Holmes's own admission when telling his own story of *The Lion's Mane*, which

> occurred after my withdrawal to my little Sussex home, when I had given myself up entirely to that soothing life of Nature for which I had so often yearned during the long years spent amid the gloom of London.

We know that Holmes's Sussex villa was situated 'upon the southern slope of the Downs'. We may therefore presume that his birthplace lay somewhere in that land of chalk cliffs and close-cropped turf; that his boyhood haunts included Eastbourne, Brighton, Hastings, and Pevensey, along the coast-line, and Lewes, Battle, and Herstmonceux inland. We know, from the fact that he was a man of sixty or thereabouts in 1914, that he must have been born about

'There's our man, Watson! Come along'

The Hound of the Baskervilles

1854. Of his schooling nothing is said, but it may be presumed that his university years were prepared for at a southern public school—Winchester at once suggests itself, for where else should the educational cradle of the young Sherlock lie, but under that grim castle on the hill, court-house and prison in one, where Dame Alice Lisle and so many other victims of cruel and misdirected laws faced their judges and their savage fate? Here, for the first time, we like to think, Sherlock's keen mind brooded on crime and punishment and justice. It was still a good place for brooding, the old cathedral city, though some sixty years had passed since Keats had commented on the excessively maiden-ladylike character of the streets, observing of their door-knockers that he "never saw so quiet a collection of Lions' and Rams' heads." In *The Copper Beeches* Holmes significantly remarks: "Had this lady who appeals to us for help gone to live in Winchester, I should never have had a fear for her."

After schooldays, the university. But which university? Much blood has flowed in scholastic wrangles as to the rival claims of Oxford and Cambridge. As we must deny ourselves the pleasure of investigating such claims—heavy as they are with evidence and counter-evidence—we will merely plump for Oxford. In spirit we have encountered Holmes in the High; we have never yet so much as caught the flutter of his undergraduate's gown in Christ's Pieces.

At Oxford, then (let us say), Holmes told Watson he spent two years.

> I was never a very sociable fellow, Watson, always rather fond of moping in my rooms and working out my own little methods of thought, so that I never mixed much with the men of my year. Bar fencing and boxing I had few athletic tastes.

However, during these withdrawn years Holmes made one friend—Victor Trevor. Trevor's bull-terrier effected

an introduction between its master and the lean and
hungry-looking young Holmes when it (somewhat short-
sightedly) fastened on to the latter's ankle one day. "It
was a prosaic way of forming a friendship," as Holmes
remarked, but Trevor proved to be as much in need of
congenial society as he was himself; and during the long
vacation Holmes accepted Trevor's invitation to spend
a month at his father's place at Donnithorpe, in
Norfolk.

This was the invitation which formed the bridge
between Holmes and high detection; for it introduced him
to Trevor Senior, and the mysterious cypher concerning
fly-paper and hen pheasants with which Holmes solved the
mystery of the *Gloria Scott*. In this youthful episode we
have our first glimpse of the great detective. Observing
old Trevor's loaded stick, Holmes deduces that he has
recently gone about in fear of some personal attack. From
the peculiar flattening and thickening of the ears, he
rightly diagnoses a past experience of boxing. From the
hands he perceives "a great deal of digging". Trevor
confirms this:

> "Made all my money at the gold-fields."
> "You have been in New Zealand."
> "Right again."
> "You have visited Japan."
> "Quite true."
> "And you have been most intimately associated with someone
> whose initials were J.A., and whom you afterwards were
> eager to entirely forget."

Mr. Trevor, moved not by the split infinitive but
by the dreadful accuracy of Holmes's diagnoses, here
falls forward on his face among the nutshells which
bestrew the tablecloth, in a dead faint. It is Sherlock
Holmes's first triumph.

Holmes admitted to Watson that this was the case which

first turned his attention to the profession which became his life's work. Before following him to London and fame, however, we must review another significant connection with the Trevor family.

It has been suggested with charm and conviction that the early love of Holmes's life, whose premature death turned him from the whole race of women, was Victor Trevor's sister. The thesis rests upon one sentence in Holmes's account to Watson of his momentous visit to Donnithorpe. "There had been a daughter, I heard, but she had died of diphtheria while on a visit to Birmingham." The apparent irrelevance, even pathos, of this statement has struck at least one biographer as significant. Was Holmes dismissing the dead Miss Trevor lightly because he could not bear to talk about her? Was he, in fact, falsifying the date of her death because he had known and loved her? Why mention diphtheria? Why particularize Birmingham?

To our minds, the answers are clear, if romantically disappointing: Holmes might have concealed a betrayal, but not, surely, a death. The man who has loved once may love again, and Holmes categorically stated to Watson: "I have never loved. . . ." We shall return to this question later, but let us regretfully re-inter Miss Trevor in her Birmingham tomb with the observation that Holmes mentioned its locality, and her complaint, because, as he said himself, it was his business to know things . . . he had trained himself to see what others overlooked. *Requiescat* Miss Trevor—'and from her fair and unpolluted flesh may *violets* spring . . .': the name-flowers of so many Holmesian heroines.

After the *Gloria Scott*, Holmes's university existence seems to have livened up, presumably because he began to try out his famous Methods about this time. "During my last years at the university there was a good deal of talk there about myself and my methods," he says. When he left university he came to London and established himself in rooms in Montague Street, just round the corner from the British Museum.

Here, in the shadow of that imposing pile, the ex-student waited for crime to come his way, "filling in my too abundant leisure time by studying all those branches of science which might make me more efficient. Now and again cases came in my way, principally through the introduction of old fellow-students."

'*Holmes was working hard over a chemical investigation*'

The Naval Treaty

Such a case was *The Musgrave Ritual*. Reginald Musgrave, who had been in Holmes's college, called on him one day with the request that he would apply "those powers with which you used to amaze us" to the "very strange doings at Hurlstone", Musgrave's Sussex home. Delighted at the chance of ending months of hated inaction, Holmes took down all details and solved the mystery of a butler's disappearance and of a curious old jingle which concealed the clue to the hiding-place of the long-lost ancient crown of England.

And now the scene was set indeed for the historic meeting. Not the Field of the Cloth of Gold itself deserved such chronicling as that occasion when, in the chemical laboratory of St. Bartholomew's Hospital, Sherlock Holmes met Dr. Watson for the first time.

Here we must pause and look back at the years which had been bringing them together. Who was Watson, what was he—and where?

John H. Watson, M.D., had been born around the mid-1850's, somewhere in the south of England. We know that during an impecunious spell in later life he yearned in the holiday season for the glades of the New Forest or the shingle of Southsea, from which a depleted bank account had temporarily debarred him. We know that on his return to England from foreign service he gravitated to London, and bitterly described it as 'that great cesspool into which all the loungers and idlers of the Empire are irresistibly drained'. This does not sound like the remark of a cockney, and we are inclined to place him as Hampshire-born, with a possibility of later residence in Surrey. We know that he had been at school with Percy ('Tadpole') Phelps, later to figure prominently in the case of *The Naval Treaty*. A suggestion that part of his boyhood had been spent in Australia we must dismiss, believing that this territory belongs to that period of his life in which he ranged over 'many nations and three separate continents', gaining experience of women. There is nothing in Watson's character, as revealed by himself, to suggest that this experience was abnormally premature, and we conclude that he took a late degree and spent part of what would have been his student days in a sort of Grand Tour—what his contemporary Jerome K. Jerome would have described as an extended Bummel.

The whereabouts of his school is uncertain. Percy Phelps's uncle was Lord Holdhurst, 'the great Conservative politician', which suggests a public school of some standing. If Holmes went to Winchester, Watson cannot have been a Wykehamist, as the two never met in boyhood.

From some deductions by Holmes about Watson's watch, we learn that this father had been dead many years in 1887 (the date of *The Sign of Four*); that Watson had had an elder brother, untidy of habits, careless, a man who had been left with good prospects but had thrown away his chances, had lived for some time in poverty with occasional short intervals of prosperity, and who had finally taken to drink and died. Watson's father's and brother's Christian name had been the same—initial H, the middle initial of Watson's own name. By 1878 the young doctor had 'neither kith nor kin in England'. Friends he had made in youth, such as Big Bob Ferguson, "the finest three-quarter Richmond ever had", to quote Watson's own opinion, had fallen away from him. An active lad, toughened in the Rugger field, simple, soldierly by nature, it was in character for him on taking his degree of Doctor of Medicine to proceed to Netley and undergo a course of training for army surgeons. There is something Kiplingesque about Watson, and in later life he must have rather resembled the poet, though possibly he grew somewhat stouter, for Bob Ferguson remarks in 1896, "You don't look quite the man you did when I threw you over the ropes into the crowd at the Old Deer Park." Watson had heard the call of the off-shore wind, and the thresh of the deep-sea rain; he had heard the song, how long, how long! Pull out on the trail again. . . . And so up with the tents of Shem, and off with the Fifth Northumberland Fusiliers, as their Assistant Surgeon. Let us hear it in Watson's own words:

> The regiment was stationed in India at the time, and before I could join it, the second Afghan war had broken out. On landing at Bombay, I learned that my corps had advanced through the passes, and was already deep in the enemy's country. I followed, however, with many other officers who were in the same situation as myself, and succeeded in reaching Candahar in safety, where I found my regiment, and at once entered upon my new duties. The campaign brought honours and promotion to many, but for me it had nothing but misfortune and disaster.

Now attached to the Berkshires, Watson served at the battle of Maiwand and 'was struck on the shoulder by a Jezail bullet, which shattered the bone and grazed the subclavian artery'. Of this, more hereafter. Rescued from death by his gallant orderly, ravaged by fever, but at last convalescent (though in his own view his health had been irretrievably ruined) Watson came home.

And so, poor, friendless, unwell, and out of a job, one morning in 1881 he drifted into the Criterion Bar for a little comfort from the cup. 'Eightpence for a glass of sherry' was the moderate charge, in those happy days, at one of London's most expensive hotels. We may presume that the Criterion let Watson off with sixpence or sevenpence. As he sipped his drink, he felt a tap on the shoulder —it was the hand of young Stamford, who had been one of his dressers at Bart's. Overjoyed at this unexpected meeting the two old friends lunched together at the Holborn. On the way they discussed Watson's search for comfortable but low-priced lodgings, and Stamford recalled that another acquaintance of his had that very day mentioned the same thing—"a fellow who is working at the chemical laboratory up at the hospital. He was bemoaning

'Then he stood before the fire'

A Scandal in Bohemia

himself this morning because he could not get someone to go halves with him in some nice rooms which he had found. . . ."

Watson leapt at this, in spite of Stamford's warning that his friend Sherlock Holmes, though a decent fellow enough, was a little queer in his ideas, and desultory and eccentric in his studies.

After lunch that day, therefore, Stamford and Watson drove round to Bart's, and there, in the lofty chamber, littered with countless bottles and illuminated by the blue flickering flames of Bunsen burners, stood a solitary student, bending over a table absorbed in his work. With a cry of pleasure—"I've found it! I've found it!"—he ran towards the advancing men, a test-tube in his hand; and then were spoken the fateful words:

"Dr. Watson, Mr. Sherlock Holmes."

Quickly they sized each other up. Watson observed of Holmes:

His very person and appearance were such as to strike the attention of the most casual observer. In height he was rather over six feet, and so excessively lean that he seemed to be considerably taller. His eyes were sharp and piercing, and his thin, hawk-like nose gave his whole expression an air of alertness and decision. His chin, too, had the prominence and squareness which mark the man of determination.

Much later, Watson was to see Holmes as 'a strange, lank bird, with dull grey plumage and a black top-knot'. His eyes shine 'with a steely glitter', and Watson mentions them frequently as 'grey'. At one moment his face seems to Watson 'that of a clear-cut classical statue'; at another he has 'the utter immobility of countenance of a Red Indian'. It is a face unforgettable, unforgotten. . . .

Within a few moments of meeting, Holmes startled

Watson by telling him that he had obviously come from Afghanistan. Later he described his train of reasoning.

> Here is a gentleman of a medical type, but with the air of a military man. Clearly an army doctor, then. He has just come from the tropics, for his face is dark, and that is not the natural tint of his skin, for his wrists are fair. He has undergone hardship and sickness, as his haggard face says clearly. His left arm has been injured. He holds it in a stiff and unnatural manner. Where in the tropics could an English army doctor have seen much hardship and got his arm wounded? Clearly in Afghanistan.

Elsewhere, Holmes refers to Watson's 'modest moustache', which judging by his best-known portraits would seem to be an under-estimation.

Drawn together perhaps by their very differences, the two young men exchanged characters, compared habits— Holmes setting off his moodiness, violin-playing and fondness for chemical experiments against Watson's laziness, irregular hours and ownership of a bull-pup. (We hear no more of this animal, and can only speculate that it succumbed to canine distemper or to the vicissitudes consequent upon life at a private hotel in the Strand, or at 221B.) The partnership was clinched, and the very next evening Watson moved his possessions round to the chosen rooms, to be followed next morning by Holmes. It was the beginning of their life at 221B, Baker Street, London West One.

Watson soon found that Holmes was the mystery Stamford had hinted he might be. ("I'll wager he learns more about you than you about him.") He was not a medical student; his knowledge was encyclopaedic in some respects and abysmally lacking in others. He seemed to be without personal friends, but received an astonishing variety of callers—a young girl, an old Jew pedlar,* a

* Could this be the unfortunate Hebrew from whom Holmes bought his Stradivarius for 55*s.*, come to demand its true price?

railway porter—alone in the communal sitting-room. "I
have to use this room as a place of business." he explained,
"and these people are my clients." We are sure that
Holmes, with that unfailing courtesy and consideration
towards women which is always evident in his dealings
with them, took Mrs. Hudson, his landlady and housekeeper, into his confidence before letting her in for this
heterogeneous procession up and down her stairs. Before

'The pipe was still between his lips'
The Man with the Twisted Lip

allowing her to take him on as a lodger, he would have
told her frankly the risks and inconveniences of doing so:
the noise of his Stradivarius, played sometimes well,
sometimes wildly, as the mood took him; his fearful
untidiness; the curious filing system which involved
securing unanswered correspondence to the mantelpiece
with a jack-knife; the keeping of cigars in the coal-scuttle
and tobacco in the toe-end of a Persian slipper; his

unorthodox hours and meal-times; and those strange visitors.

Obviously, Mrs. Hudson minded none of it. A presumed widow of respectable status, she may well have had that attraction to the exotic which is shared by so many people who are themselves the souls of conventionality. Perhaps the departed Hudson had been a Bit of a One, and she missed him. At any rate, we know from Watson that Mrs. Hudson stood in awe of Holmes, and never dared to interfere with him, however outrageous his proceedings might seem. She was fond of him, too; no doubt his ascetic appearance brought out all that was motherly in her nature. She loved to feed him well, reflecting that but for her he would probably never eat at all, poor man. 'The very worst tenant in London' he may have been in theory, but his good-natured landlady would not have recognized him by such a description.

On the 4th of March, when the two men had settled down comfortably together, Watson happened to pick up at breakfast a magazine article entitled *The Book of Life*, which purported to show how an observant man might learn by an accurate and systematic examination of all that came his way. It struck Watson as a remarkable mixture of shrewdness and absurdity, and he said as much to Holmes, who was eating toast. Indeed, he went so far as to describe the article as rubbish and ineffable twaddle. Holmes, no doubt finishing his toast first, calmly announced that he had written it himself, and for the first time disclosed to Watson his true profession.

> I'm a consulting detective, if you can understand what that is. Here in London we have lots of Government detectives and lots of private ones. When these fellows are at fault, they come to me, and I manage to put them on the right scent. They lay all the evidence before me, and I am generally able, by the help of my knowledge of the history of crime, to set them straight.

Before Watson had fairly had time to digest this information—or his breakfast—there came a loud knock, a deep voice below, and by the hand of a retired sergeant of Marines was delivered a large blue envelope addressed to Mr. Sherlock Holmes. It was from Mr. Tobias Gregson, 'the smartest of the Scotland Yarders', remarked Holmes, and it began: 'There has been a bad business during the night at 3, Lauriston Gardens, off the Brixton Road. . . .'

Holmes had been summoned to help. Should he go? He was not sure—if he did, Gregson, Lestrade & Co., would pocket the credit. But on the whole he thought he would go, if only to laugh at them.

"Get your hat."
"You wish me to come?"
"Yes, if you have nothing better to do."

'A minute later,' says Watson, 'we were both in a hansom, driving furiously for the Brixton Road'. The curtain had gone up on *A Study in Scarlet*, and on seventeen years of a most remarkable double act.

For those who wish to read of the famous Cases, we have summarized them and their characters elsewhere. We are here concerned only with the detective and his chronicler—for this was Watson's role, to which his actual profession came second. "I am lost without my Boswell!" exclaims Holmes. "You are the stormy petrel of crime, Watson." And Watson says of himself, a little pathetically:

I was a whetstone for his mind. I stimulated him. He liked to think aloud in my presence . . . if I irritated him by a certain methodical slowness in my mentality, that irritation served only to make his own flame-like intuitions and impressions flash up the more vividly and swiftly.

Sometimes Holmes was irritated by Watson's slowness of mind; sometimes he laughed at him, though kindly. "Excellent, Watson! Compound of the Busy Bee and Excelsior." But they complemented each other perfectly, and although Holmes complained that Watson over-romanticized and embellished too much the cases which he chronicled, he must have known perfectly well that without Watson they would never have been chronicled at all. Many, indeed, never were—perhaps because not even Watson could entirely neglect all his patients all the time, and there is only so much time in the world for a man to write. 'Somewhere in the vaults of the bank of Cox & Company, at Charing Cross, there is a travel-worn and battered tin dispatch-box with my name . . . painted upon the lid,' says Watson. 'It is crammed with papers, nearly all of which are records of problems which Mr. Sherlock Holmes had at various times to examine.' For various reasons, he adds, these cases have not been made public. We fear that now they never will be, and the loss is ours. What really happened to Mr. James Phillimore, who, stepping back into his own house to get his umbrella, was never more seen in this world? How did Isadora Persano come to be found stark staring mad with a matchbox in front of him which contained a remarkable worm, said to be unknown to science? What was the Adventure of Ricoletti of the Club Foot and his Abominable Wife? And the Repulsive Story of the Red Leech? And the Case of Wilson, the Notorious Canary Trainer? Our appetites have been whetted, but we shall never have them satisfied.

We cannot entirely rely on Watson's dating of the stories which he has recorded: his facts we do not question too closely, but his chronology is undoubtedly rocky. Other commentators have analysed fully the extraordinary contradictions in date which beset the seeker after Watsonian truth. It is all of a piece with his remarkable vagueness on other matters.* Where in fact, was the

---

* His own name, for example. Like A. A. Milne's raindrops

> 'Both of him had different names:
> One was John and one was James.'

bullet-wound which pained him on damp and windy days?
'In one of my limbs,' he says evasively in *The Noble
Bachelor. The Sign of Four* finds him 'nursing my wounded
leg. I had had a Jezail bullet through it some time before.
. . .' And 'What was I, an Army surgeon with a weak
leg and a weaker banking account. . . .' But the very first
account that he gives of himself states that 'I was struck
on the *shoulder* by a Jezail bullet, which shattered the bone
and grazed the subclavian artery.' It is very puzzling. We
are forced to conclude that Watson received *two* (or more)
bullets during the Afghan campaign, and, brave man that
he was, thought one of them not worth chronicling at the
time.

But although there is no certain proof as to which
wound earned him that pension, half of which went on
racing (so that Holmes had to keep his cheque-book
locked up, in trust for him) we are inclined to believe that
the major injury was in his leg; for there is Holmes's
unimpeachable testimony to it in the sentence: "A six-
mile limp for a half-pay officer with a damaged *tendo
Achillis.*"

According to Holmes, Watson has another Heel of
Achilles: Women. "Now, Watson," he says jocularly, "the
fair sex is *your* department." And even more pointedly:

> With your natural advantages, Watson, every lady is your
> helper and accomplice. What about the girl at the post office,
> or the wife of the greengrocer? I can picture you whispering
> soft nothings with the young lady at the 'Blue Anchor', and
> receiving hard somethings in exchange.

But was this more than friendly rallying? We doubt it.
Apart from Watson's astonishing statement about his
tri-continental experience of women, there is nothing in
his own admissions to confirm this reputation; unless one
is to take seriously his early remark to Holmes in connection with his laziness and irregular breakfast-times:

"I have another set of vices when I'm well, but those are the principal ones at present." No, no, good easy man, he referred only to betting and gambling.

There is something distinctly inexperienced, naïve, and touchingly youthful about the way in which this supposed Casanova of Baker Street reacted to his first meeting with Miss Mary Morstan. The heroine of *The Sign of Four* was a small, neat, blonde of twenty-seven, who entered Holmes's rooms wearing a costume of plain simplicity with a suggestion of limited means about it. Her little grey-beige turban was relieved 'only by a suspicion of white feather in the side'. Her features were not regular, her complexion not striking, but her sweet, amiable expression and large blue eyes caused the startled Watson to call upon his famous experience of women, adding that in all of it he had never looked upon a face which gave a clearer promise of a refined and sensitive nature. He was done for, clean bowled. It was love at first sight; an honourable love that withdrew its pretensions when Miss Morstan proved to be a potential heiress. It was the love of a romantic, simple, and intensely honest young man, respectful to a degree. As they stood with Holmes outside the sinister bulk of Pondicherry House, their hands, Watson admitted afterwards

> instinctively sought for each other. I have marvelled at it since, but at the time it seemed the most natural thing that I should go out to her so, and, as she has often told me, there was in her also the instinct to turn to me for comfort and protection. So we stood hand-in-hand, like two children . . .

So overcome with emotion had Watson been on the drive to Pondicherry Lodge that in his attempts to cheer and amuse Miss Morstan with tales of his adventures in Afghanistan, he included one moving anecdote as to how a musket looked into his tent at the dead of night, and how he fired a double-barrelled tiger cub at it. He was, in fact, completely *boulversé* with love, and it was a kindly Fate which sent the Agra Treasure to the bottom of the Thames and set Watson free to take Mary's undowered little hand in his for life.

Though not, alas, for a long life. Their brief, happy marriage was to end with her death in little more than four years.

But that is still to come. At the satisfactory conclusion of *The Sign of Four* Holmes said some extremely complimentary things about Watson's wife-to-be, but added hastily:

> ... love is an emotional thing, and whatever is emotional is opposed to that cold, true reason which I place above all things. I should never marry myself, lest I bias my judgment.

And he reached out his long white hand for the cocaine-bottle which Watson so rightly deplored.

It is not surprising that Watson developed an unshakeable conviction that Holmes was cold, unemotional, a bloodless fish, who disliked and distrusted women. He liked to scatter 'shock' remarks such as that quoted above, partly to get a rise out of the simple Watson and partly because he was obviously deeply afraid of love itself, and the effect it might have on the great passion of his life— detection. We believe he spoke the truth when he said: "I have never loved, Watson." But he went on to say that if he had loved a woman who had died as Brenda Tregennis (of *The Devil's Foot*) had died, he might have avenged her as Brenda's lover did.

There is ample evidence in the Cases that he liked women, was at ease with them, handled them charmingly, dealt with them chivalrously and kindly, and knew a great deal about them. There is not one instance of his treating a woman rudely or harshly. Even when interrupted by Miss Violet Smith, the Solitary Cyclist, at a moment when he was immersed in a very abstruse and complicated problem, he spared her a weary smile, gave her a seat, and within a few moments was turning her face gently towards the light and telling Watson that it had the spirituality of a musician. Of poor worried Mrs. Neville St. Clair, waiting at The Cedars for news of her missing husband, he speculated to Watson on what he should say "to this dear little woman tonight when she meets me at the door". Hardly the thoughts of a misogynist.

To the landlady, Mrs. Warren (of *The Red Circle*), he was a miracle-worker who had brought light into the darkness for a lodger of hers. She came to Holmes when in doubt and darkness herself, almost hysterical. Holmes

> laid his long, thin fingers upon the woman's shoulder. He had an almost hypnotic power of soothing when he wished. The scared look faded from her eyes, and her agitated features smoothed into their usual commonplace.

It was Holmes's sympathetic wisdom that saved the terribly scarred Eugenia Ronder from suicide. He argued in passionate sincerity with the proud, beautiful Violet de Merville, in an attempt to make her give up her depraved lover, and thought of her, he says, "as I would have thought of a daughter of my own". As for the famous Irene Adler—'to Holmes she was always *the* woman', although—nay, because—she defeated and tricked him. With the swagger and panache of a Shakespearean heroine, she resorted to male costume in order to mock Holmes at his own door, calling a saucy good-night in the guise of a slim youth in an ulster. Her mocking letter to him, at the end of the case of *A Scandal in Bohemia*, is the salute of one great personality to another, its worthy antagonist. Even the rather unadmirable King of Bohemia, who had been using Holmes to extract a compromising photograph from the lady, was forced to exclaim: "What a woman—oh, what a woman! . . . Would she not have

made an admirable queen? Is it not a pity she was not on
my level?"

"From what I have seen of the lady, she seems, indeed, to
be on a very different level to Your Majesty," replied Holmes
coldly.

We may follow the king's thought a little further, and
speculate: Would she not have made an admirable partner
for Holmes, either marital or in the way of business? He
must have recognized this, for to him even her photograph
was rated above emeralds, and stood for ever in the place
of honour upon his mantelpiece.

Less romantic, but equally significant of Holmes's
relations with The Sex, is the episode of the Hampstead
Housemaid. Having tried all obvious means of getting at
Charles Augustus Milverton, the blackmailer, without
success, Holmes was inspired to disguise himself as a
rakish young workman with a goatee beard and a swagger,
and in this Jovian transformation to get engaged to
Milverton's housemaid, Agatha: a gambit which called
forth from Watson the shocked cry: "Good heavens,
Holmes!"

Representing himself as 'a plumber with a rising
business, Escott by name', Holmes walked and talked
with the susceptible girl, won her heart, and incidentally
extracted enough information from her to enable him to
burgle Milverton's house. "But the girl, Holmes?" protested Watson. Holmes shrugged.

You can't help it, my dear Watson. You must play your cards
as best you can when such a stake is on the table. However, I
rejoice to say that I have a hated rival who will certainly cut
me out the instant that my back is turned.

It is the only instance of Holmes behaving unchival-
rously to a woman in all the pages of Watson's chronicles;
and after all it was in chivalry's cause, for he acted on

behalf of Lady Eva Brackwell, 'the most beautiful debutante of last season', whose future lay in the dirty hands
of Milverton. We are sure that he knew he had not broken
Agatha's heart; but we think it was probably more than a
little dented. 'He had a remarkable gentleness and
courtesy in his dealings with women,' says Watson,
obtusely.

Indeed, Watson's obtuseness about Holmes's inner life
was astonishing. Upon Holmes's unusually emotional
apology for exposing Watson to the dangers of the dreadful Devil's Foot vapour, Watson observed that he had
never seen so much of Holmes's heart before. And in his
concern for Watson's wound during the case of *The Three
Garridebs*, the surprised Watson 'caught a glimpse of a
great heart as well as of a great brain'. Although he
recorded one of Holmes's most significant remarks (made
to Alexander Holder of *Beryl Coronet* fame) he failed to
see the light cast by it on his friend's great hidden mind:
"You owe a very humble apology," Holmes had said
sternly to Holder, "to that noble lad, your son, who has
carried himself in this matter as I should be proud to see
my own son do, *should I ever chance to have one*." The line
has a pathos which could not have come from the born
bachelor portrayed by Watson.

But there is much to forgive Watson, considering the
preoccupations that beset him. In 1887 he married Mary
Morstan; at some time between 1891 and 1894 she died.
We do not know why she should have died so young (in
her early thirties). Perhaps it was a case of the all too
common pulmonary T.B., for her frequent absences from
home ('on a visit to her aunt's' or simply 'away on a visit')
suggest prolonged spells at a sanatorium. Whatever the
cause of her death, it was too painful for Watson to
chronicle.

Mary died during Holmes's absence from London, after
his supposed death in the dreadful Reichenbach Falls,

locked in a final struggle with his great enemy, Moriarty.
Watson, doubly bereaved but retaining the stiff upper lip
of a soldier and a gentleman, carried on with his profession
and with his hobby of trying to solve reported crimes by
Holmes's own methods. His life must have been very
barren. When, in the adventure of *The Empty House,*

*'Sherlock Holmes was standing smiling at me across
my study table'*
The Empty House

Holmes magically reappeared in the disguise of a shabby
old book-collector, Watson fainted as much from joy as
from shock. The rooms at Baker Street had been preserved
intact by Mycroft Holmes, who was in the secret of his
survival. Mrs. Hudson, poor soul, had not been taken into
Mycroft's confidence, and on the return of her late lodger

from the grave very naturally fell into violent hysterics. So, in an atmosphere of general rejoicing and reunion, the great partnership began once more, although in a modified form.

Soon after his marriage Watson had left Baker Street and bought a practice in Paddington, near the station. (There is, or used to be, an enchanting little house in Sale Place, off Praed Street, with its façade set off by a graceful wreathing vine, which we have often envisaged as the home of Watson and Mary.) As his practice increased, his connection with Holmes grew weaker, and in 1890, the year before the Reichenbach affair, he only recorded three of Holmes's cases. He had always been ready to leave his patients to his accommodating neighbours, Drs. Anstruther and Jackson, at the call of the Master Mind, and many a note had been scribbled to Mary explaining that her husband had again thrown in his lot with Holmes. But in spite of this, doctoring must have grown upon Watson. Though never highly imaginative, he had a warm and confidence-inspiring personality, and what he did know he probably knew well. "My practice is never very absorbing," he had said in earlier days; but it had gained more of a hold upon him than he realized. During Holmes's absence he had taken a small practice in Kensington (which he afterwards sold at top price to a young doctor named Verner, who proved to be a relation of Holmes—Holmes, in fact, had anonymously put up the money for the purchase).

By 1902 Watson had moved to his own rooms in Queen Anne Street, off Harley Street, the most fashionable doctors' quarter, and a considerable step-up from his previous terrain. In 1903 Holmes, telling his own story of *The Blanched Soldier*, remarks that in January of that year 'the good Watson had . . . deserted me for a wife, the only selfish action which I can recall in our association. I was alone.'

This can only refer to a second marriage made by
Watson, some ten years after his first wife's death. He
himself makes no reference to it; perhaps because the
second Mrs. Watson objected to figuring in the Chronicles.
We know nothing about her, but there is a hint somewhere—perhaps in the very absence of detail—that she
was a less sympathetic character than Mary. Holmes had
not considered Watson's first marriage 'selfish' because
Mary had never stood in the way of Watson's partnership
with him. The inference is obvious.

It has been suggested by previous biographers that
Mrs. Watson II was Violet de Merville, that cold,
spiritual beauty whom Holmes saved from a disastrous
marriage with the vile Baron Gruner. Beautiful she may
have been, with 'the ethereal other-world beauty of some
fanatic whose thoughts are set on high', but there her
attractions seem to have ended. Holmes records drily that
"she waved us into our respective chairs like a reverend
abbess receiving two rather leprous mendicants. If your
head is inclined to swell, Watson, take a course of Miss
Violet de Merville".

We cannot seriously imagine that Watson followed his
advice. If Watson's tastes are to be judged by Mary
Morstan, they lay in the direction of much cosier women
than Miss de Merville. Nor would she have been likely to
favour the simple, honest doctor. If 'every woman is at
heart a rake', as Pope surmised, it should follow that the
most virtuous women must be irresistibly attracted by the
worst men. If the dreadful business of Baron Gruner did
not teach Violet de Merville a lesson, she may well have
taken up with yet another villain whom she confidently
expected to reform; or else have forsworn men altogether
and given herself up to the relentless pursuit of good works.

Twice married, middle-aged, comfortably prosperous,
with work of his own to interest him, Watson never completely forsook Holmes. Any suggestion that the later

A common loafer
The Beryl Coronet

*A simple minded
clergyman*
A Scandal in Bohemia

'My decrepit Italian friend'
The Final Problem

A drunken-looking groom
A Scandal in Bohemia

SHERLOCK HOLMES IN VARIOUS DISGUISES

Cases are recorded by another hand—that of a ghost-Watson, in the literary sense—may be dismissed. If they lack some of the pungency of the earlier ones, it is understandable in view of Watson's new preoccupations, and of a possible increase in his tendency to vagueness about dates. We see the two friends still together until 1903, though no longer under the same roof. A deep understanding must have grown up between them by now. Holmes had mellowed, had perhaps become wiser in the ways of living. He had benefited under Watson's kindly care and we hear no more of morphine or of the seven-percent solution of cocaine which had once solaced his times of inactivity, or of days without food. The 'iron constitution' to which Watson had so often admiringly referred was beginning to show signs of wear after some twenty years of demoniacal treatment by its master. Rest-cures in Cornwall and elsewhere had never been very protracted, interrupted as they always were by some conveniently sited crime. Food and drink, for which he had always had a connoisseur's palate, seem to have been of particular interest to Holmes in his later years. In *The Hound of the Baskervilles* (1889) he was satisfied enough while in hiding on the Moor by 'a loaf of bread and a clean collar', but the balance was restored at the end of the case by 'a little dinner at Marcini's'. In his last Watsonian case, *The Creeping Man*, he refers with deep interest to that inn called the 'Chequers' at Camford where 'the port used to be above mediocrity, and the linen was above reproach'. In the last Case of all, *His Last Bow*, in fact, comes that glowing tribute to the bottle of Imperial Tokay—that 'remarkable wine' from Franz Joseph's special cellar at the Schoenbrunn Palace. ("Might I trouble you to open the window, for chloroform vapour does not help the palate.") And we note that on leaving the scene of Von Bork's arrest Holmes returned to his London base—'at Claridge's Hotel'.

It was during the affair of *The Creeping Man* that Holmes, furious with himself at not having seen earlier the significance of Professor Presbury's horny hands, grasped his forehead and cried:

> Oh, Watson, Watson, what a fool I have been! . . . All points in one direction. How could I miss seeing the connection of ideas? Those knuckles—how could I have passed those knuckles? And the dog! And the ivy! It's surely time that I disappeared into that little farm of my dreams.

By the end of the same year he had done so. When the Case of *The Lion's Mane* (related by himself) begins, we find him in

> my little Sussex home, when I had given myself up entirely to that soothing life of Nature for which I had so often yearned during the long years spent amid the gloom of London. At this period of my life the good Watson had passed almost beyond my ken. An occasional week-end visit was the most that I ever saw of him.

This home of Holmes was a villa commanding a great view of the Channel, near the little cove and village of Fulworth. Here, attended only by his old housekeeper— probably, but not certainly, Mrs. Hudson—he kept bees, and worked on 'the magnum opus of my latter years': a *Practical Handbook of Bee Culture, with some Observations upon the Segregation of the Queen*. To produce this, he spent 'pensive nights and laborious days' watching 'the little working gangs as once I watched the criminal world of London'. He had softened sufficiently to speculate of the lovely Miss Maud Bellamy of Fulworth:

> Who could have imagined that so rare a flower would grow from such a root and in such an atmosphere? . . . I could not look upon her perfect clear-cut face, with all the soft freshness of the Downlands in her delicate colouring, without realizing that no young man would cross her path unscathed.

And no ageing one, possibly. We have always felt it was a near thing for Holmes's housekeeper that his neighbours did not include some charming widow or farmer's sister of somewhat riper years than Miss Bellamy.

The Sussex squires had reasserted themselves in him; the Vernets, whose art had taken such a strange form in the blood of their descendant, had stepped back into the shadows.

Only once again did Holmes forsake his country retreat for the old, thrilling game. It was 1912. England's Premier and Foreign Minister personally besought the retired Master to set out on the trail of the elusive German agent Von Bork. It took him two years of roughing it, mainly in America, before he managed to insinuate himself into Von Bork's English household in the guise of an Irish-American motor expert called Altamont, an Uncle Sam-like figure—accompanied by his chauffeur, a heavily built, elderly man with a grey moustache.

Yes, it was Watson—'the one fixed point in a changing age'. Together they triumphed over Von Bork, revelled in Franz Joseph's Imperial Tokay, and gazed over the moonlit sea, while Holmes prophesied the coming of an east wind, "such a wind as never blew on England yet. It will be cold and bitter, Watson, and a good many of us may wither before its blast".

We cannot think that either Holmes or Watson withered before it. Nor east wind nor age can wither them, though they are now into their second century. As they are immortals, there is no particular need to search too closely for their epitaphs; but, should they for any academic reason be sought, Holmes has written them. Of himself:

> I think that I may go so far as to say,
> Watson,
> That I have not lived wholly in vain.
> If my record were closed tonight
> I could still survey it with equanimity.

The air of London is the sweeter for my presence:
In over a thousand cases
I am not aware that I have ever used
My powers upon the wrong side.

And of his faithful friend, ally and recorder:

Watson,
You excel yourself.
I am bound to say that in all the accounts
Which you have been so good as to give
Of my own small achievements,
You have habitually underrated
Your own abilities.
It may be that you are not yourself
Luminous,
But you are
A Conductor of Light.

SIR ARTHUR CONAN DOYLE

A rt was in the blood of the first son of Charles Doyle, Deputy Head of Her Majesty's Office of Works in Edinburgh, when he arrived in the world on May 22nd, 1859: and it was to take some singular forms.

Previously, art in the Doyle family blood had meant Art. Charles, who would remain a Civil Servant all his working life, had been drawing and painting exquisitely since his childhood. His brother Richard had illustrated Dickens and Thackeray and designed the famous cover which was to serve for the best part of a century the magazine in which so many of his drawings appeared, *Punch*. Another brother, Henry, was a professional artist and Director of the National Art Gallery, Dublin. Their father's eminence was even greater. Drawing under the initials, 'H.B.', John Doyle was the leading political caricaturist of his time.

The family was an old-established Irish squirearchy with a familiar story of gradual eviction from its lands. John Doyle's wife had been Marianna Conan. When Charles Doyle and his Irish-born wife, Mary, asked Uncle Michael Conan, editor of a Parisian art review, to be godfather to their first son, he forwarded with his acceptance a copy of a new book, *Arthur de Bretagne*, about a Conan ancestor; and thus the name Arthur Conan Doyle came to be pronounced at the christening.

Apart from the infusion of art in the blood, Arthur, like many other sons of his time, was to owe more to his mother than to the male side of his parentage. She was a proud, dogmatic woman, a descendant through her mother of the Percys of Northumberland, with a passion for the nobility of history, which she soon began to impress upon her child in the form of tales of chivalry and stirring deeds. Throughout her life, which was long, she remained his confidante, example and adviser; and, more particularly, the agent of his inspiration for some of his finest works.

Godfather Michael suggested a Jesuit education for the

son of generations of Catholics, and Arthur was sent to Stonyhurst. Academically, he came to owe less to his tutors than to his own efforts. Formal lessons held little interest for him, compared with the self-discovered works of Scott, Macaulay and other romantic employers of history for their own ends. Nobody was more surprised than he when he passed his matriculation with honours. At the age of sixteen he left Stonyhurst for a year at Feldkirch College, in Austria, where his incidental discoveries included two which were to join prominently in those influences already at work in him: Napoleon and Edgar Allan Poe.

He enjoyed excellent health; he was a keen sportsman, physically active and courageous; he was, in spite of himself, a fine scholar. The combination suggested a career: medicine. He joined the Medical Faculty of Edinburgh University in 1876—and met the man who was to provide a major part of the conception of Sherlock Holmes.

Dr. Joseph Bell believed not only in teaching his students surgery; it was his delight to impress upon them constantly the fact that, given a practised alertness of eyes, ears and brain, a diagnosis could commence from the moment a patient came through the door. Arthur Conan Doyle was fascinated to hear him demonstrate: and when, in *The Greek Interpreter*, Sherlock and Mycroft Holmes turn on for Watson's benefit their virtuoso display of perception and deduction, we hear the art of Dr. Bell epitomized:

"An old soldier, I perceive," said Sherlock.
"And very recently discharged," remarked the brother.
"Served in India, I see."
"And a non-commissioned officer."
"Royal Artillery, I fancy," said Sherlock.
"And a widower."
"But with a child."
"Children, my dear boy, children."

This sort of thing, however, was yet to come. Arthur Conan Doyle's immediate preoccupation was to find some means of helping to pay for his studies and his keep. His father's income, even with the extra he could make as a spare-time illustrator, was meagre, and his health was deteriorating. Arthur's obvious source of a little income was to offer his services during vacations to any general practitioner needing assistance. There was little response and less money. As a schoolboy he had tried his hand at writing—poems, mostly—but now he tried a short story, *The Mystery of Sasassa Valley*. He was delighted when *Chambers' Journal* accepted it and paid him three guineas; but further stories with which he endeavoured to follow up this success were all rejected.

He had already considered, when qualified, becoming a Naval surgeon, and now, still a student and badly in need of money, he was able to sign on as 'surgeon'—a nominal appointment involving a seaman's duties with recourse to his special knowledge in case of emergency—aboard the 600-ton steam whaler, *Hope*. The adventure took him to the Arctic and back, and left him with a much-needed £50. He graduated as Bachelor of Medicine and Master of Surgery in 1881, and returned to the sea for a brief stint, this time on a passenger liner to West Africa.

The first offer of a practice ashore came from a happy-go-lucky friend named Budd, formerly bankrupt but now prosperously established in Plymouth. Boasting of 30,000 patients and above £4,000 takings in a year, Budd offered Doyle a share—all visiting, surgery and midwifery, with a guaranteed income of £300 in his first year. The offer, too good to refuse, was accepted. The details of life with Budd can be read in the largely autobiographical novel *The Stark Munro Letters*. But the partnership did not endure. The Ma'am, as Arthur always referred to his mother, disapproved of Budd and said so in her letters, some of which Budd and his wife found lying about. The aggrieved benefactor suggested that his protégé might like to set himself up in practice elsewhere, offering him £1 a week to help him. Arthur plumped for the Portsmouth suburb of Southsea, where a house was going cheap, bought at an auction enough furniture to equip his consulting room adequately and his living quarters meagrely, and put up his brass plate—which he had to sneak out and polish after dark, since domestic help was out of the question. Dr. Budd thereupon withdrew his £1 a week, and Dr. Arthur Conan Doyle was left to fend for himself; though not quite for himself, for the Ma'am had despatched his ten-year-old brother Innes to live in and provide the necessary 'front' as page-boy. Another of Innes's duties was to keep a Log of the day's doings, from which the following is an extract:

> This morning after breakfast Arthur went downstairs and began to write a story about a man with three eyes, while I was up stairs enventing a new water-works that will send rokets over the moon in two minutes and they will send small shot at the same distance then it was a quarter past one, so, I had to go and put on the last potatoes the only six we had in the world.

The situation was not quite desperate. Patients were beginning to call, some of them no doubt attracted not so much by the new doctor's reputation as a physician but as a sportsman. He was already achieving local distinction at cricket, football and bowls. Grateful patients added to the household furnishings. Even so, progress was disappointing; and this was how Fate meant it to be, for had Arthur Conan Doyle's practice developed as spectacularly as Budd's had done he could scarcely have found time or incentive to hammer away, as he now did, with adventure stories, for which a variety of journals contributed a few guineas every now and again. A self-applied test of his ability as a writer was to try to get a story into *The*

Cornhill, then the most respected journal of its kind. He achieved the ambition in 1883 with a story based on the *Mary Celeste* mystery, entitled *Habakuk Jephson's Statement*, published, unsigned, the following year. There were revealing repercussions. Her Majesty's Advocate-General at Gibraltar read the story, mistook the fiction for purported fact, denounced it publicly as untrue, and provided its author with a great deal of publicity and the knowledge that, like Poe, he could write a story so convincingly that it no longer appeared to belong to imagination, but to reality. Even so, success was far from assured. Most of what he wrote continued to be rejected. But he kept at it and started his first novel, *Girdlestone & Co.*

Indeed, Dr. Conan Doyle now felt confident enough to marry. His bride was Louise Hawkins, ('Touie') the sister of one of his patients. And now, casting about for a new subject for his writings, it occurred to him to write a novel about a detective.

Fergus Hume wrote *The Mystery of a Hansom Cab*, which enjoyed sensational sales in the late 1880's, after reading the works of Emile Gaboriau. When Conan Doyle read Hume's novel he found it disappointing: perhaps because Gaboriau had already set in motion a train of thought of his own. Very much to his taste were the methods of the French author's shrewd detective, Lecoq, whose use of logical synthesis, bold experiment and carefully studied disguise made him a fictional peer of a profession whose practice had scarcely begun to be formulated in real life. Little wonder that Conan Doyle's thoughts should have returned at this time to the methods of Dr. Joseph Bell. If only these could be applied to the detection of crime: and they could. Like Hume (whose novel had not yet appeared) he began with a hansom cab; only he did not concern himself with its occupant, but with the cabbie himself—a man who, say he were a potential murderer, might travel freely about London without suspicion as to

his movements or his motives for them. *A Tangled Skein*
was to be the title and the story would be told by one
Ormond Sacker: but wait—that name would not do.
Something less fanciful was needed. Something less fanciful
was to hand. James H. Watson was the name of a young
doctor friend of his at Southsea. To avoid possible
embarrassment the James was changed to John, and of an
immortal pair, Watson was the first-born. As for the
detective who would bring the application of exact
sciences to criminology, making it an exact science in its
own right: Sherrinford Holmes? No, not quite. As the
author pondered, his Irish background prompted an Irish
name: Sherlock—Sherlock Holmes.

The publishers who might have had the honour of
launching the most famous character in English literature
upon the world declined it. *A Study in Scarlet*, as the story
had now become, was rejected by *The Cornhill* as being too
long for a single story and too short for a serial. Two
other publishing firms also rejected it. It found a taker at
length in the firm of Ward, Lock & Co., who accepted it
for later publication in a Christmas annual. Undiscerning
though publishers had proved themselves, the author, too,
had no conception of the eventual stature of the character
he had created. He accepted £25 for the outright sale of
the copyright. He would have preferred a royalty basis;
but the offer was the best he had had, and the work would
at least now reach the public.

Meanwhile, he was off upon a very different tack. With
A Study in Scarlet still awaiting publication he began, in
1887, to plan his first historical romance, *Micah Clarke*.
He wrote it in three months and embodied in it all that he
knew of the seventeenth century and all that he had
learned from Scott and Macaulay of the art of bringing
history to life upon the printed page. Again, the publishing
world proved unresponsive. *Micah Clarke* spent a year
doing the rounds. *A Study in Scarlet* appeared in *Beeton's*

Christmas Annual for 1887 and created no stir. At last *Micah Clarke* found a home with Longmans, who published it in February, 1889, shortly after the birth of the Conan Doyles' first child, a daughter, Mary Louise. The critics who had failed to notice Holmes and Watson fell upon Micah with enthusiasm. Arthur Conan Doyle knew from that moment that his doctoring days would soon be left behind.

Meanwhile, he turned his mind to a subject for a further historical novel: and now there came to the surface of his consciousness the true recognition of the spirit of chivalry which his mother had never ceased to implant in him throughout his boyhood. It emerged not as a likely theme for a new story with which to consolidate the beginnings of literary and commercial success, but as a code for living, embraced so instinctively and sincerely that from the start the new project burned with its light. *The White Company*, however, was anything but a work of pure and simple fervour. Months of study of the England of the Middle Ages were required before the story began gradually to take shape. And while the people of 1366 were one by one assuming substance in the author's mind, Sherlock Holmes once more insinuated himself into life. In response to a request by the American editor of *Lippincott's Magazine*, a new novel, *The Sign of the Four*, as it was originally entitled, was written quickly and published simultaneously in England and America in February, 1890.

But the main task in hand remained *The White Company*. In July the author hurled his pen across the room, splashing the wall-paper with ink, and cried: "That's done it!" By the time it had completed its appearance as a serial in *The Cornhill* and been reissued as a book, Arthur Conan Doyle had left Southsea, had all but turned his back upon medical practice, and had conceived a Machiavellian notion to kill off Sherlock Holmes.

After a period in Vienna, he had written—between
15*

April and August, 1891—six Sherlock Holmes stories, beginning with *A Scandal in Bohemia*, which had been tentatively submitted through an agent to George Newnes's latest magazine, *The Strand*. Their success had been immediate. The public, and the editor, clamoured for more. Conan Doyle refused. A new historical novel, *The Refugees*, set in Canada, was occupying his mind. The editor persisted. Hesitating between the demands of income and a labour of love, the author decided to resolve the matter by asking the outrageous fee of £50 each, irrespective of length, for six more Holmes adventures, and to abide by the response. His terms were accepted by return of post and once again the feet of Holmes's clients were heard upon the stair.

In addition to the novels *A Study in Scarlet* and *The Sign of Four*, twelve short stories now existed, enough to make up a book with the title *The Adventures of Sherlock Holmes*, which, the author confessed, seemed no bad notion. But, as ever, Holmes was getting in the way of more 'serious' work: he must be marked down for what his creator considered a timely end. The Ma'am had other ideas. Holmes must be allowed to live. Bowing to her insistence—and incorporating some of her suggestions— Conan Doyle completed the series with Holmes being told (in *The Copper Beeches*) that his skill had never risen to such heights.

His hand, however, was only temporarily stayed. Pressed for still more Holmes stories he again sought release by asking an exorbitant fee—£1,000 for twelve tales. To his wonder the proposal was accepted. Doyle wrote the twelve and then summoned up his resolve, entitled the last of them *The Final Problem*, and sent Holmes and Moriarty plunging together into the Reichenbach Falls.

By the time this disastrous narrative burst upon the public (who responded with vituperative letters and the wearing of mourning bands) Conan Doyle had become preoccupied with sorrows of his own, of all too real a nature. His father had died in October, 1893. Touie, suddenly stricken, had been given a matter of months to live before consumption claimed her. 'We must take what Fate sends,' he wrote to the Ma'am; but he resolved to fight a delaying action with Fate by taking his wife to the Swiss Alps in the hope that the climate would bring about some improvement. There he wrote *The Stark Munro Letters* and, incidentally, introduced the sport of skiing, with imported Norwegian skis. Touie's health did improve and he was able to bring her back to England in the late spring of 1894 and accept an offer to tour the United States, reading selections from his works. His American hearers took to him as he took to them. 'The race as a whole is not only the most prosperous, but the most even-tempered, tolerant, and hopeful that I have ever known,' he wrote to the Ma'am. To buoy him up against the strain of travel and overpowering hospitality there arrived cables reporting the immediate success back home of his stage play *Waterloo*, with Irving as the veteran Corporal Gregory Brewster.

Napoleon and his wars were in the forefront of Arthur Conan Doyle's mind as he returned, weary but elated, from his American visit. With customary thoroughness he had for several years been steeping himself in their literature. He read his first Brigadier Gerard story to an American audience, and back in Switzerland, where Touie awaited him, he managed almost to complete the seven further stories to comprise *The Exploits of Brigadier Gerard*. Once more he had created a character so real, against a background so vivid, that what he had written seemed scarcely fiction at all. He achieved the same illusion in *Rodney Stone*, his next novel, the prize-fighting tale set in England during these same Napoleonic times.

Now, from re-creating conflicts of olden times, Arthur

Conan Doyle was to come face to face with war in his own day. On October 11th, 1899, the protracted unrest between Boers and British in South Africa flamed up into a state of war. While his latest play, *Sherlock Holmes*, with the uncannily Holmes-like American actor William Gillette in the title role, was being acclaimed a dramatic triumph in the U.S.A., its author was volunteering for service. He was refused, but was at once accepted by his friend John Langman as senior physician (unpaid) of the privately endowed Langman Hospital, preparing for front-line service.

The Langman Hospital was seemingly well equipped. But the enteric fever epidemic which followed Christian de Wet's capture of the waterworks near Bloemfontein soon showed up its weaknesses. In the face of desperate overcrowding it ran short of disinfectants, linen and other basic supplies. Worse still, the morale of most of its senior staff crumbled under pressure. Conan Doyle assumed charge and fought the epidemic with two junior surgeons and a devoted band of orderlies, one quarter of whom were themselves overcome by it. When respite came at last and he found time to muse upon the crass stupidity of the British military leaders, whose inability after the long peace of Victoria's reign to set aside traditional methods of warfare and adapt their tactics to the needs of the moment had made possible such unnecessary losses as that of the waterworks, he wrote an article proposing reforms which were to infuriate the die-hards but would become necessities before the passage of little more than a decade. British bravery was no longer enough. Warfare had become no longer the exclusive concern of well-drilled professionals. "Let us have done with the fuss and the feathers, the gold lace and the frippery! Let us have done also with the tailoring, the too-luxurious habits of the mess, the unnecessary extravagance which makes it so hard for a poor man to accept a commission! If only this good came from all our trials and our efforts, they would be well worth all that they have cost us."

For all his personal labours he had found additional time and strength to study objectively the progress and lessons of the tragic campaign, still not officially ended. His book *The Great Boer War*, published soon after his return to England, stated the case and reported the deeds of both sides with a frank impartiality which earned the popular author of detective fiction and historical romance a new respect, to which he was shortly to add with a passionate work of 60,000 words, *The War in South Africa: Its Cause and Conduct*. While not hesitating to castigate his own side where castigation was required, he spoke up with all the vigour at his command in defence of the maligned, un-championed British Tommy against the baseless charges of barbarism, rape and murder which had enjoyed unchallenged currency both abroad and at home. Even this new-found popularity and the *cachet* of having, soon after his return, played for the M.C.C. at Lord's, was not sufficient, however, to translate him from private to public life. As he had done once before, he stood for Parliament and was defeated. There was not enough dissimulation in him for a politician; but the Mother of Parliaments undoubtedly missed some stirring, if disturbing speeches.

But what of Sherlock Holmes during this period of private public service? During his toils amongst the sick and the dying in South Africa, Conan Doyle had rightly displayed short patience towards such interviewers as had tactlessly insinuated questions about Holmes among graver matters. Holmes, to all intents and purposes, lay dead, somewhere beneath the torrents of Reichenbach.

In March, 1901, Conan Doyle rested at Cromer, in Norfolk, seeking to rid his system of the after-effects of enteric fever and his mind of the turbulence of war-sufferings. There he played golf with a friend, Fletcher

Robinson; and there, one wet afternoon, he lazed before a comforting fire while Robinson rambled on about Dartmoor, its legends, and, in particular, a spectral hound. Early April found Conan Doyle on Dartmoor himself, the plan for 'a little book', to be entitled *The Hound of the Baskervilles*, already in his mind. As he had conceived it, Sherlock Holmes had no part in this tale. Nevertheless, a good story-teller willingly accepts the dictates of his own pen, and having given way to the insistence of a character as determined as himself, Conan Doyle had to console himself with the assertion that the adventure constituted an isolated incident, hitherto un-chronicled, from Holmes's past life.

Holmes may have been dead, but, like the character in the Gracie Fields song, he certainly had no intention of lying down. In September, 1901, while readers of *The Strand* panted in anticipation of the next episode of *The Hound*, William Gillette repeated at the Lyceum Theatre, in London, his American success with the stage play *Sherlock Holmes*. Two more years passed. Then, also from America, in 1903 came an offer—a plea, almost—which could not be gainsaid. If Conan Doyle could find some means of bringing back Holmes alive, five thousand dollars per story would be forthcoming. George Newnes, sensing also, perhaps, that it was now or never, offered something over half this sum for the English rights. Arthur Conan Doyle took up his pen and wrote a postcard to his agent: 'Very well, A.C.D.' And into Watson's doubly bereaved life there sidled a seedy bookseller, who, while his back was momentarily turned, effected a transformation which sent the good doctor into a faint and set the British public clamouring at the bookstalls.

Contrary to belief in some quarters at the time, Conan Doyle's knighthood was not bestowed upon him as the creator of Sherlock Holmes. The honour, for services to his country, had come (and might have been refused, but for the Ma'am's insistence that refusal would have been an insult to the King) in 1902, the year in which, it will be recalled, Holmes declined the same honour. Even this mark of public recognition was not sufficient to sway the electorate. At Joseph Chamberlain's request Sir Arthur Conan Doyle made one more bid for a seat in Parliament and was defeated. As in everything, he tried his best; but politics could scarcely occupy the upmost part of his mind in competition with a new undertaking in historical literature. In writing *Sir Nigel* he returned to the theme and period—and some of the characters—of *The White Company*: England in the days of chivalry, with Nigel Loring as a poor boy, aspiring to manhood and the realization of the ideals set before him by the regal old Dame Ermyntrude, with her tales of knightly honour and derring-do. To his disappointment, the new book was not acclaimed as his greatest work, although it earned much praise and big sales. He had already achieved, seventeen years before, more than he had perhaps realized with *The White Company. Sir Nigel* could only be complementary to it.

In 1893, Touie had been given a few months to live. Now, in 1906, she died. Nearly thirteen years' reprieve detracted nothing from the blow to her husband. For the first time in his life he fell seriously ill. Reaction, after years of concern and hard work, dragged him down into an uncharacteristic torpor. He slept badly. No eager projects claimed his attention: until one day he picked up a bundle of press-cuttings, placed upon his desk by his secretary, and Sherlock Holmes, the resented character, became Sherlock Holmes, the man.

Conan Doyle's personal fight to establish the innocence of a Parsee, George Edalji, convicted of sheep-maiming in Warwickshire has been recounted at length elsewhere, and, regretfully, there is not space to re-tell it here.[*] Sensing that an injustice had been perpetrated upon a

---

[*] See *The Life of Sir Arthur Conan Doyle*, by John Dickson Carr (John Murray).

defenceless victim, he girded on that same sword with which he had smitten down those who had found the inarticulate Tommy Atkins an easy target for their accusations. On that occasion, public opinion had quickly shown him its support. Now, he was up against the vindictiveness of prejudiced police officials, the apathy of anyone to whom the sufferings of a Parsee solicitor were of no concern, and the calculated obtuseness of a Government which could not bring itself to admit unreservedly that an error had been made and an innocent man wronged. With much help from some quarters of the press, Conan Doyle finally got his way, not merely by the persistence of his representations, but by investigating the evidence against George Edalji, proving it to be defective, and actually claiming to have discovered the real culprit (who, however, was never brought to trial, nor his name revealed). It was a real-life Sherlock Holmesian case, solved by a real-life Sherlock Holmes. And it was not the last experience of its kind for the man who, while never admitting publicly to self-identification with his famous detective, was not above providing some strong hints in the stories. Within a few years he was fighting again with the same tenacity and methods and for the same general principles, only this time the immediate stakes were higher. The wrongful conviction was for murder. The victim of persecution and suppression of evidence was again a man of foreign origins, living in Britain, secure, it might have been presumed, under the protective cloak of British justice. His name was Oscar Slater.* Conan Doyle took up his case—

* See *The Trial of Oscar Slater,* edited by William Roughead (William Hodge & Co.). The Slater and Edalji investigations were by no means the only ones undertaken in this way. The immense unpublished Conan Doyle archives, which in so many ways are the counterpart of Holmes's own archives, contain references to a number of other criminal cases in which Sir Arthur took a practical hand.

reluctantly—in 1911. It took him until 1927 to win it. This was no impulsive fighter, quick to anger and equally quick to cool. He not only argued and wrote on Slater's behalf: he contributed thousands of pounds towards the cost and support of this German Jew, of unsympathetic manner and tainted background. His reward was a note from Slater: 'Sir Conan Doyle, you breaker of my shackles, you lover of truth for justice sake, I thank you from the bottom of my heart for the goodness you have shown towards me. . . .'

Apart from these criminal cases, the years before the first world war saw another instance of Conan Doyle's compulsion to fight injustice wherever he found it. *The Crime of the Congo*, his 'booklet' of 60,000 words, published in 1909, was a damning exposure of ill-treatment, murder and exploitation by Belgian administrators and traders of the people of the Congo Free State. As with *The War in South Africa: its Cause and Conduct*, not a penny earned by the huge sales at home and abroad of this shocking document went into its author's pocket. This was not a literary enterprise, but a crusade.

In 1907 Conan Doyle had married Jean Leckie, the inheritor of a Scottish lineage as long and romantic as his Irish one. They had loved one another almost from their first meeting in 1897. They were to have three children —Denis (1909), Adrian (1910), and Jean (1912); and there were two of Touie's—Mary and Kingsley, both well into their teens.

Nothing halted the progress of his writing. In 1909, in the face of discouraging advice from all sides, he took on the lease of the Adelphi Theatre, in London, in order to present his spectacular drama of Regency England, *The House of Temperley*, which, in its great prize-fighting scene, carried stage realism to a pitch which had the audience in the aisles. It was far from a complete success, running for only four months, against the hoped-for minimum of six; but Sherlock Holmes was waiting in the wings for his cue to leap to the rescue. A stage version of *The Speckled Band* soon had houses packed again.

Having tried to kill Holmes, and failed singularly, Conan Doyle had no doubt learned by now to accept philosophically the inevitability of letting him live on unmenaced. Although his literary inclinations lay elsewhere, he was too much of a professional to insist on denying his public what it wanted from him, so long as there should remain time and energy to tackle other work when he wished. In any case, he had conceived an antidote to Holmes, a character as flamboyant as Brigadier Gerard, as consistent as Holmes, and as life-like and immediately acceptable as either of them—Professor Challenger. Not surprisingly, Challenger quickly became his creator's own favourite. Rampaging through *The Lost World*, doing and saying whatever came to his mind, irrespective of conventional usage or the social niceties, Challenger, through sheer noise and exuberance, eclipsed the quietly irrepressible Holmes—in the eyes, at least, of the author: the public, while they took to Challenger with a will, sacrificed to him none of their loyalty to Holmes, and in any popularity contest posterity would have no doubt which way to vote.

The pre-war years were among the most taxing of Conan Doyle's life. In addition to all else, we find him embracing such causes as divorce law reform, Home Rule for Ireland, the Channel Tunnel, and the raising of a strong British team for the next Olympic Games. There were bigger and graver preoccupations, too: the need for increased food production at home, import tariffs, and the frustrating task of endeavouring to convince the British Government that, in German hands, the aeroplane and the submarine were potential menaces to the life of the nation. He had little doubt about the inevitability of war. He had travelled too widely, been admitted to too many con-

fidences to believe anything else. Driven by his belief in
the urgency of the situation, he campaigned incessantly
for the better training of Territorial reservists (he himself
had introduced the first Rifle Clubs into the country after
the South African War); he issued warnings about the
potential dangers of floating mines at sea; he returned
again and again to the menace of the submarine, and, with
the outbreak of war only a few months away, wrote a long
short-story, *Danger! Being the Log of Captain John Sirius*,
a remarkable prophecy of how the war at sea would be
fought.

Before the war, with its new tasks and tragedies, could
engulf him, he turned yet again to Sherlock Holmes and
wrote the last of the four detective novels, *The Valley of
Fear*. 'I fancy this is my swan-song in fiction,' he wrote
to the editor of the *Strand*. What he really meant was that
it was the last time he expected to have to write anything
other than of his own choosing. As usual, he was wrong.
Holmes was to take his last bow yet.

Conan Doyle was in his mid-fifties when war broke out.
Although the War Office would not accept his offer to
serve again as a front-line doctor, he was to have plenty
to occupy him. He formed the first Volunteer Battalion,
the forerunners of the Home Guard of a later war, and
served in it as a private; he saw his prophecies of submarine warfare come true, and campaigned, in vain, for
the supply to all ships of inflatable rubber dinghies; he
read of futile bayonet attacks against machine-guns,
experimented in his garden, firing bullets at sheets of
different metals, and sent in his recommendations for the
provision of steel helmets and heart-shields to British
troops; he toured the front in France, found that tactics
and practices which he had been attacked for advocating
at the time of the Boer War were now in common use;
and, musing upon the slaughter about him, he found
himself—the former Catholic and agnostic—convinced

beyond any further doubt of the existence of that life after death which he had been studying without personal commitment for over twenty years.

Sir Arthur Conan Doyle's pursuit of the truth of Spiritualism, his sudden passage from scepticism to belief, and the subsequent long and difficult campaign he waged across many countries to bring his convictions to others, is, like some other aspects of his life upon which we have merely touched, a subject needing separate and unstinting consideration. He wrote: "All other work which I had ever done, or could ever do, was as nothing compared to this." And, as though to test his new faith, death took from him, at the war's very end, his son Kingsley and his brother—Conan Doyle's former page-boy in buttons of the Southsea days—Brigadier-General Innes Conan Doyle; and then, within another two years, the Ma'am. His belief never faltered. The last decade of his life was to be devoted almost completely to his new cause, with an occasional story—generally with a supernatural element—as a gesture towards his faithful readers of the *Strand*.

He died on July 7th, 1930. He was buried in the grounds of his house in Sussex. There was no mourning: like the characters he had invoked from out of the air, made to move and talk, and, finally, laid aside, he had lived but would never die.